Time and time again I have benefited from reading or listening to what Justin has to say about making disciples. He not only thinks deeply on this subject but also provides many practical insights and applications for those who want to be obedient to the great commission.

CHRIS KOVAC, pastor of outreach ministries, West Highland Church

A short but powerful little book that's full of wisdom and practical advice from real-life practitioners in the church trying to make disciples. . . . Very useful for churches trying to make the paradigm shift from church growth (seeker-sensitive nonsense) to obeying Jesus by fulfilling the great commission.

BRETT RICLEY, associate pastor of discipleship and adult ministries at The Mission Church

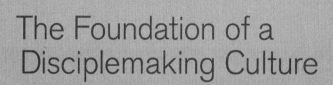

The Foundation of a
Disciplemaking Culture

BUILDING A CORE TEAM
TO AWAKEN A MOVEMENT

JUSTIN G. GRAVITT

A NavPress resource published in alliance
with Tyndale House Publishers

NavPress.com

The Foundation of a Disciplemaking Culture: Building a CORE Team to Awaken a Movement

Copyright © 2024 by Justin G. Gravitt. All rights reserved.

A NavPress resource published in alliance with Tyndale House Publishers

First edition copyright © 2020 by Justin G. Gravitt

The Team:
David Zimmerman, Publisher; Linda Washington, Copyeditor; Olivia Eldredge, Operations Manager; Jennifer L. Phelps, Designer

For information about special discounts for bulk purchases, please contact Tyndale House Publishers at csresponse@tyndale.com, or call 1-855-277-9400.

ISBN 978-1-64158-741-9

Printed in the United States of America

30	29	28	27	26	25	24
7	6	5	4	3	2	1

Contents

Preface

Now more than ever, information is cheap. The internet is a warehouse of information that robots can now deliver with human-like interaction. Such effortless knowledge (artificial intelligence) tempts us to believe that knowing is an adequate stand-in for becoming. The problem is that there is a big gap between information and transformation.

For centuries Christian maturity has been defined (in large part) by knowing. For years, I relied on books to grant me the feeling of learning and growth; but without application, my voracious reading was really just entertainment. I was educated by books, but I wasn't deeply formed by them.

While books by themselves can't form us into disciples, disciplemaking relationships invite us into a space where another Christ-follower can see us—weaknesses and all—and speak into who we can become as we follow the King.

In that respect, using a book to learn any aspect of disciplemaking is a bit of an oxymoron. Jesus' way of making disciples presupposes incarnation: presence that is face-to-face and life-on-life. In disciplemaking, nothing can ever replace really seeing another person.

No book, no matter how well written, can ever do that.

So why write about this topic? Why do we need another book adding to the overwhelming reams of written words already out there?

It's still true that while the fields are ripe for harvest, "the laborers are few."[1] If there were enough people actively engaged in making disciples, then we'd each have someone with the vision, heart, and skill to walk alongside us as we learn how to make disciples who make disciples. If you have someone like that, lean into that relationship as you read this book together to supplement what you're already doing. If you don't have someone like that, then this book is also for you.

This book is especially aimed at Christian leaders, including pastors. I admire your commitment to the local and global church. My prayer is that what follows will help you develop a CORE team, which is the solid foundation from which to build a disciplemaking culture.[2]

FOUNDATION PROBLEMS

"Suppose one of you wants to build a tower. Won't you first sit down and estimate the cost to see if you have enough money to complete it? For if you lay the foundation and are not able to finish it, everyone who sees it will ridicule you."
JESUS, LUKE 14:28-29

Bonanno Pisano was a man of great vision. This twelfth-century sculptor combined physical strength and patience with an intricate eye for detail—widely diverse skills that the work of a sculptor required. Such an artisan is always in demand. Leaders of cities across the region would invite him to complete projects that would bring status to their cities and enhance their legacies. Time and time again, Pisano delivered the highest quality craftsmanship with superior artistic perspective and detail. He was a remarkable sculptor, a man of great vision, calling forth vivid images from stone and bronze.

What prompted the famous sculptor to try his hand at architecture is a mystery. Perhaps it was ego or simply an inability to say no, but whatever the reason, on August 9, 1173, Pisano started building a tower that would become the defining project of his life. Launched with funding from an opera-house widow, the tower was to be part of a great cathedral complex and would stand as a sign to the nations of his hometown's grandeur. As the white building rose straight and true, the residents of Pisa watched with pride.

The first person to notice the tilt is a mystery too: It could have been a local laborer, a visiting professional, or perhaps even a child. But in 1178, after nearly five years of steady progress, some observant soul pointed out that the tower seemed to be leaning, ever so slightly, to the south.

The drama that ensued from that one simple observation has been lost to history, but it's easy to imagine. That person told another who told another until word reached Bonanno Pisano. Of course, he wouldn't have believed it at first. The very idea likely offended him. After all, the now two-story tower had been straight as an arrow since he'd laid the foundation over four years earlier. But an accusation that serious forced him to walk away from the tower and take a good, long look to see for himself.

The tower was indeed leaning.

Pisano's "crooked-tower moment" did to him what it would do to most people. He was devastated and embarrassed. News of the lean traveled fast. His city was trying to grow its reputation, but his leaning tower would be mocked instead of admired. How could this have happened?

Instead of rising to the height of his expectations, the tower revealed the level of his training. Pisano had skill, clear vision, and commitment, but he had missed something important: The problem was with the foundation—and it was too big for him to fix. He abandoned the tower and hoped history wouldn't remember his mistake.

Today the Leaning Tower of Pisa is a world-famous landmark. At the time, however, it was a cautionary tale. How had such a critical problem hidden itself from view for over four years? What could be done about it? The leaders of this Italian city would wrestle with those questions for the next eight hundred years.

The story of the Leaning Tower of Pisa is a textbook example of the impact of a foundation problem. But it's far from the only one. In Pisa alone, there are two other towers that lean. Outside Pisa, the world has dozens of unintentionally leaning towers, including London's Big Ben and San Francisco's Millennium Tower.

The Leaning Tower of Pisa holds many lessons for architects, engineers, and city planners—and yes, even disciplemaking leaders.

A Solid Foundation for Disciplemaking

Architecture and church leadership may seem miles apart, but each one demands careful planning and execution in order to withstand the challenges that are sure to come. Disciplemaking leaders must learn to lay a foundation that won't sink or shift over time.

A strong foundation is vitally important because without one, leaders risk the same outcome Pisano experienced—rapid growth masquerading as progress before eventually falling in on itself. What remains in the rubble are broken promises, loads of unrecoverable time, and the leader's confidence. Whether the problem is recognized as an embarrassing "crooked-tower moment" or a full implosion, rebuilding is not an easy task.

Many leaders have learned the hard way that disciplemaking can appear to thrive—for years, even—yet still fail to develop into a disciplemaking culture. Pastor Norm is one of those leaders. Years into faithful leadership of his church, Pastor Norm decided they needed more intentional discipleship. He found a resource he liked and started investing in some men on Tuesday mornings. Six months later he asked them to go and do the same. And they did! The next year his church of three hundred had over fifteen discipleship groups. Pastor Norm and the elders were thrilled that their dedication to disciplemaking had so quickly yielded such great results.

Four years after the first group, Pastor Norm had his crooked-tower moment. For the first time, the total number of discipleship groups declined. The decline continued year after year and led to a full-on collapse.

Something had gone terribly wrong. Upon investigation, they learned what it was: People would participate in a group, then lead a group, and then most would simply opt out. The replication of groups, it turns out, wasn't a reliable indicator of individual transformation. Instead of making disciples of Jesus, church members were simply making disciples of the discipleship curriculum.

Pastor Norm was crushed. He didn't know what to do or what to conclude. Was it disciplemaking that didn't work? Was it his fault? Had he missed something? With no one to turn to, he couldn't be sure. Within a few short months, discipleship at the church reverted to what it was before Pastor Norm started his first group. In his discouragement he decided to return to what he was sure of: preaching and shepherding. Everyone had meant well, but without the necessary foundation, the illusion of progress destroyed Norm's confidence in himself as a disciplemaker and in disciplemaking as an effective ministry.

Norm's story isn't unique. This is the story of many church and ministry leaders—the story of trusting in "the next thing" to make disciples, a story of hope that ends in deep disappointment.

The bad news is that the next thing almost never works. The good news is that next-thing thinking isn't the only way. There's a better way.

For disciplemaking to last in your church or ministry, it needs to be part of the DNA of your church or ministry culture. For that to happen, you will need to build a disciplemaking foundation. A disciplemaking culture isn't "the next thing"—it's the first thing, the thing that will finally put all the next things into their proper place.

Understanding that is easy. Building a disciplemaking culture is incredibly costly. But it's also worth it.

Defining Terms

Words are the tools we use to communicate ideas, and when they are uncared for, they rust. Rusty words cannot accomplish the job of clear communication. And clear communication is foundational to every culture-making effort.

Disciplemaking words have been used carelessly for decades and are full of rust. Many church and ministry leaders use words like *disciple*, *discipleship*, and *disciplemaking* in loose, inconsistent, and often completely unrelated ways. Instead of bringing clarity, they have become a source of confusion and frustration. To foster good communication throughout this book and in your own disciplemaking culture, I will define key terms. (See also appendix A.)

> **Disciple:** Someone who follows Jesus in order to become just like Jesus, is being changed by Jesus, and is committed to the mission of Jesus.

Note the contrast with the dictionary definition of *disciple*: "One who accepts and assists in spreading the doctrines of another."[1] Our definition of *disciple* tethers the term to the gospel and helps distinguish between people who merely agree with Jesus' teachings and those who actively strive to embody those teachings. It speaks to *motivation*: To become just like Jesus is what motivates a disciple; it anchors the act of following Jesus to a fixed goal.

The phrase *being changed by Jesus* acknowledges the mysterious relationship between our efforts and Jesus' transformative work in us. The phrase *committed to the mission of Jesus* reminds us that there is work to be done. We are to pursue those who don't know Jesus.[2] Taken together, our definition is broad enough to include brand-new disciples of Jesus and those who have been following Him for decades. Everyone is called to be a disciple.

> **Discipleship:** The process of helping a disciple grow to Christlike maturity—minus intentional movement toward making other disciples.

The word *discipleship* has been nearly devoured with rust; this definition aims to free it. *Discipleship* has become the contemporary church's Swiss Army–knife term for anything and everything.

It's typically used synonymously with *disciplemaking*, though both terms deserve conceptual independence from each other.

Usually, *discipleship* refers to anything that helps someone grow as a disciple (events, classes, workshops, etc.), but it can also refer to relational settings (small groups, cohorts, mentoring, triads, even one-on-one relationships). No matter what the setting, the focus of discipleship is usually on helping disciples grow. As the definition here reflects, discipleship typically does not include orienting disciples toward disciplemaking.

Because of the extreme rust on the word *discipleship*, I rarely use it.

Defining *Disciplemaking*

That brings us to *disciplemaking*. A short discussion is needed before we define this word, since clarity is imperative for building a disciplemaking foundation and culture. What is disciplemaking?

- Is disciplemaking simply "doing deliberate spiritual good to help [someone] follow Christ," as one leading pastor suggests?[3]

- Is disciplemaking "everything the church does," as another pastor told me?

- Is disciplemaking "something that only God can do," as a faithful Christ-follower once told me?

- Is disciplemaking merely leadership development, as a misreading of Jesus' words and actions in Mark 3:14-15 and Matthew 28:18-20 might indicate?

Perhaps the bigger, more challenging question is this: Is it possible to define *disciplemaking* in a way that captures the essence of Jesus' command to His disciples: "Go and make disciples of all nations"?[4] Can such a definition exist without denigrating the other work of the Kingdom?

Let's start by acknowledging three truths that complicate the matter.

1. God has given us the job of making disciples.[5]
2. God ultimately is the One who causes disciples to grow.[6]
3. Disciples can be made effectively in many ways.

The challenge of clearly communicating about disciplemaking revolves around these three truths and the half-truths that often grow out of them. To protect against those half-truths, let's agree on three things:

First, since God gave us the job of making disciples, let's agree that we can do it. But let's also acknowledge that we can only do it as we abide in Him.[7] It would be outside God's character to give us a job that we couldn't do in partnership with the Holy Spirit.

Second, even if we don't abide in Christ, we can expect mature disciples to emerge from every church or ministry. This is the result of the Spirit's work in the lives of individual believers.[8] It's easy to see why many believe only God can make disciples, especially since this second truth shows that He does the heavy lifting! Many leaders are misled by the presence of mature disciples in their church or ministry, but mature disciples are *always* part of God's grace to a congregation. They are only *sometimes* the result of intentional ministry. Leaders must remember that the mere development of mature disciples does not necessarily indicate effective disciplemaking. Mature disciples could emerge because of what you (and God) did, in spite of what you did, or for reasons unrelated to what you did.

Third, since there are many ways to make a disciple, careful thought must be given to *how* we make a disciple. This is especially important because disciples will *go in the same ways they have grown*. In other words, the way a disciple is made is the way that disciple will naturally go to make disciples in the future. So *how* a disciple is made is critically important.

A disciplemaker's choices will impact generations of disciples. The same principle is at work in parenting. This is why so many of us wake up one day to realize that we've become our father or mother! Normally such a comforting (or disturbing) insight comes all of a sudden as we are actively parenting our own children. Our choices impact not only those we disciple but also those they will disciple and the ones *they* will disciple—for generations.

I don't point this out to raise your anxiety, but to raise your intentionality. Our calling is too high to engage in haphazard disciplemaking. Fortunately, the example Jesus set can anchor our intentionality. Put simply, *Jesus' way of making disciples is the best way*.

Jesus-Style Disciplemaking

The Scriptures teach us that Jesus' life *and* ministry are examples for us to follow.[9] Since Jesus' way is the best way, our goal isn't simply to make disciples, but to make disciples in a manner consistent with Jesus' example. Sadly, many fail to make disciples because their imitation of Jesus ends at His morals. However, as pastor and author Jim Putman often says, "We cannot separate the teachings of Jesus from the methods of Jesus and expect to get the results of Jesus."

Let's acknowledge that there's a practical limit to our imitation. In over twenty-five years of disciplemaking, I've yet to meet someone who travels with twelve disciples day and night from place to place. It's not the exact form or experience of disciplemaking that we seek to emulate, but rather the principles that undergird His method and point us toward His style. Jesus' method of disciplemaking becomes the fixed point from which we can consider the validity of all possible (and potentially effective) ways to make a disciple.

There is wide agreement that the eight principles laid out in Robert E. Coleman's classic book *The Master Plan of Evangelism*[10] represent Jesus' disciplemaking style well.[11] Those principles are frequently condensed to three: *relational, intentional,* and *missional.*

In that light, let's define *disciplemaking*:

1. *The motivation.* Disciplemaking is a specific type of relationship carried out by individuals whose *primary motivation* is being like Jesus (the Christological motivation), participating in the promise made to Abraham in Genesis 12 (the covenantal motivation), or reaching the nations in an expansion of God's Kingdom (the missional motivation).

   Motivation is important because *why* we do something makes a difference in *how* we do it and *how long* we will do it (more on this in chapter 2). Each of these motivations puts God and His plan at the center (not us), and each one also incorporates a strong personal reason to disciple others.

2. *The methods.* Disciplemaking must be carried out with *methods* that are relational, intentional, and missional. This is Jesus' way, which is the best way. We can expect disciplemaking relationships to become warped when we do not align our methods with His.

   The motivation to replace Jesus' methods with other methods is often driven by a desire for greater speed, scale, and efficiency. However, replacing relationship with programs, ongoing intentionality with events, and mission with meeting needs simply doesn't produce the same results.

3. *The multiplication.* Disciplemaking always leads to *multiplication.* The multiplying fruit of disciplemaking produces new disciples (converts), new disciplemakers, and a three-dimensional momentum. If disciplemaking never reaches the lost, then it doesn't follow Jesus' style, because Jesus came "to seek and to save the lost."[12] Jesus' disciples embodied that priority as they went. If disciplemaking doesn't produce new disciplemakers, it misses the essential element of becoming like Jesus in a holistic sense. Jesus made disciples, so to become like Him is to go and do likewise. Finally, Jesus' style of disciplemaking produces momentum that moves (1) out toward the lost, (2) in toward the church, and (3) down into the life of the individual believer. The body of Christ is built up and expanded by this momentum.[13]

   The result of this multiplicative orientation of disciplemaking is generations of disciples who move freely across social, racial, economic, or political boundaries.

To sum up, then, **disciplemaking** can be defined as follows:

> A specific type of relationship carried out by people who are primarily motivated by Christological, covenantal, or missional aims, using Jesus' methods that are relational, intentional, and missional. The relationship leads to fruit that multiplies in the form of new disciples, new disciplemakers, and momentum in three dimensions: (1) out toward the lost, (2) in toward the church, and (3) down into the life of the individual disciple.

This definition is specific enough to provide a framework from which to assess whether or not something really fits Jesus' style of disciplemaking. At the same time, it's broad enough to include various forms of disciplemaking such as a very small group of five all the way down to one-on-one disciplemaking.

Such a definition does not exclude or denigrate those who disagree, but rather provides common language and a common target toward which we can all move.

Derived from that definition are the following:

Disciplemaker (or Discipler/Reproducing Disciple/ Multiplying Disciple/Laborer): A disciple who is motivated by Christological, covenantal, or missional aims to help at least one other disciple become like Jesus by following Jesus, being changed by Jesus, and joining the mission of Jesus. Being a disciplemaker is marked by relationship, intentionality, and mission, and it continues until the one being discipled becomes an experienced disciplemaker.

Every disciple of Jesus is called to grow into a disciplemaker. In addition to Matthew 4:19 and 28:19-20, Luke 6:40 makes this abundantly clear: "The student is not above the teacher, but everyone who is fully trained will be like their teacher."

Jesus-Style Disciplemaking: Disciplemaking that seeks to replicate in today's world the principles used by Jesus in making disciples.

These definitions will aid communication throughout the following chapters. Next, we'll turn our attention to defining a disciplemaking culture and learning why it's worth the cost.

Reflection Questions

1. Have you ever experienced a crooked-tower moment in ministry? What did you learn from it?

2. What definitions of *discipleship*, *disciple*, and *disciplemaking* have you previously used (if any)?

3. How would accepting that "Jesus' way of making disciples is the best way" make defining and evaluating disciplemaking easier?

4. What parts of the disciplemaking definition stand out most to you? Why?

5. Communicate what you've discovered to God. What next step is He asking you to take?

BUILD A DISCIPLEMAKING CULTURE?

America's best churches don't have a discipleship program or "ministry," but a disciplemaking culture and identity.
THE BARNA GROUP WITH THE NAVIGATORS, *THE STATE OF DISCIPLESHIP*

"A *disciplemaking culture*? What is that?" No one should be surprised at the confusion this phrase causes. Its two main concepts, *disciplemaking* and *culture*, are famously difficult to pin down. Since we already chased down a robust definition of *disciplemaking*, let's tackle what's meant by *culture*, and then we'll clarify what we mean by *disciplemaking culture*.

What Is Culture?

Discussing culture can feel a bit like hosting a late-night infomercial—"But wait, there's more!" Culture saturates everything. It influences the thoughts people think, the decisions they make, and the directions they resist. I'm not suggesting culture is all-powerful, but it *is* inescapable. When humans come together, there is no such thing as a cultural vacuum. We carry culture with us. When we connect, we cannot *not* create culture.

As all-encompassing as culture is, not one of the 727,969 words in the New International Version is the word *culture*. At the same time, there's not a single verse in Scripture that isn't dripping with culture. Not. One.

For this book, I have chosen the following definition of **culture**:

> A population's way of life. It includes the shared language, beliefs, values, stories, history, practices, and habits of a people. It's what most of the people believe, think, and do most of the time. It forms the (mostly invisible) operating system for that population.

Journalist Walter Lippmann once defined *culture* as the "climate" of a civilization.[1] That's helpful because like climates, culture is always experienced but seldom obvious. Culture is a population's way of life. It includes the language people speak, but it also includes *how* people express their ideas and emotions in different situations.

Culture is the canvas upon which we paint. It's the operating system that guides our lives. It's the water in which we swim and the fabric with which we sew. Think these statements are hyperbolic? Consider the impact the dominant religion of a place has on its inhabitants. In Thailand, where Buddhism is by far the dominant religion, believing that each person has many lives is common. In America, where Christianity continues to dominate religious life, the normal belief is that we each have one life. People in these countries typically carry these beliefs regardless of whether they follow the rest of the religion.

Consider the impact that one belief might have on how a person engages their life. What difference would it make to live in a place where relationships and fun are more important than hard work and accomplishment? Wouldn't that deeply mark how a person engages his life and work? How he sees himself and others?

Culture is built from the collective values and beliefs of a group. It takes into account their stories and history, their normal behavior and practices, their preferred modes of communication and impartation of the group's beliefs and values—all these things and more. Culture is about what is real right now and what is going to be real in the future.

Disciplemaking Culture

A disciplemaking culture is a population who has intentionally formed an identity around being disciples of Jesus and making disciples using the methods of Jesus. Disciplemaking is a key part of the culture's DNA.

Not long ago, I joined some of the world's top disciplemakers from multiple organizations for a few days of connection and discussion. One activity we did together was to list ways of measuring the health of a disciplemaking culture. In just fifteen minutes, my group of four had listed fifteen distinct markers. It's not that we were finished; our time was up! I still have that list, but it's not very helpful because it's incomplete—as any such list would be. Describing what a disciplemaking culture looks and feels like is far more effective.

Disciplemaking cultures are like fingerprints—as distinct as the people who have them. This is as it should be. God created us with diversity in gifting, personality, and story. While every disciplemaking culture is unique, some similarities—like the arch, loop, and whorl of fingerprints—can be observed. So I will try my hand at painting three such portraits. As I do, imagine each one within your framework.

Portrait 1—Ownership and Initiative

One day you are returning from a leadership meeting, and you see two messages on your phone. The first is from Tim, who is moderately involved in your ministry. You don't know him well, but he clearly looks up to you as a leader. He asks for prayer because his close friend Ben was just diagnosed with an aggressive form of cancer. At the end of the call, you hear his voice quiver with emotion as he gets out his specific request. "I don't know, could you just pray for me? For wisdom, I guess . . . and, of course, for Ben's healing." You feel the heaviness of the situation and wonder what else you need to do for Tim, and whether God might open up a door for you to minister to Tim.

Like most leaders, your plate is already full, but sometimes things come up that need your attention. You decide to pray right away for Tim, Ben, and the whole situation. As you say amen, you are still wondering if you need to schedule some time with Tim.

Next, you listen to the second message. It's from Adam, one of your leaders. His message starts, "Hey, I just got a call from Tim. I'm not sure if you've heard, but he's really struggling.

Ben, a friend of his from work, has cancer, and it doesn't look good. Worse yet, Ben doesn't know Jesus. I think Tim is in a dark place. I'm going to get over there today to talk with him. I'll just try to encourage him, and if it makes sense, I'll help him develop a plan of how to care for Ben and share Jesus with him. Anyway, super heavy stuff. I'll circle back and let you know how it goes. Bye."

Three months later, Tim helps Ben surrender to Jesus; a month later, Ben gets to meet his Lord in heaven.

Portrait 2—Connection and Generations

Last year, Zach and Andrea Shilt, a couple in their midthirties, joined your church. You see them frequently and enjoy talking with them as well as with their eight-year-old son and five-year-old daughter. They are members of the hospitality team, and you love how faithful they are. Every week you know you'll see them, even if they are a few minutes late after getting the kids dressed, fed, and out the door.

A couple of weeks after returning from a trip, you notice the Shilt family is missing. You ask Dan, the hospitality team coordinator. He says, "Oh yeah, that's a good question. I noticed they haven't been on the schedule. Let me ask Allen and Mary Beth. They've been discipling them." After the service, Dan finds you and says, "Hey, I talked to Allen, and he said the Shilts are doing great. They went to a destination wedding for Zach's sister. They should be back next week. Oh, and Allen said that Zach is discipling someone and that Andrea is praying about discipling someone as well. Pretty cool, huh?"

Portrait 3—Grace and Care

"Hey [you], I'm looking forward to our review of the year tonight."

"Yeah, me too," you say, but inside you are only looking forward to it because it's in the future! You've been running on fumes lately, and the thought of criticism feels as horrible as a root canal.

The meeting begins with the positives—like these meetings always do. You nod in agreement as the church board happily recognizes that while attendance has remained steady, there were twice as many new Christians and 60 percent more disciplemaking relationships compared with the previous year. There have been a lot of struggles over the past few years to get to this point, but fruit is finally starting to show. You know you should feel joy like the others, but instead, you just feel a slight sense of relief.

Next the meeting shifts to "growth opportunities." Thankfully the group concludes that what's needed is to simply continue what the church has already been doing. You nod in agreement. Then Ed, the most senior person, turns to you and says, "But there is one other thing. We are concerned about you."

You straighten in your chair and say, "Oh? Why? I'm doing fine. Things are going well, right?"

"Yes, but we've noticed your morale isn't what it used to be. You're still getting everything done, but—and I don't know exactly how to say it—you just seem different, like muted somewhat. We think you need a break. You've been here nine years now, and we realized you haven't taken any time for extended rest. So in the next year, we want you to take a six-week sabbatical."

That sounds amazing to you, but you're concerned about what those who aren't in the room will think. You're sure most won't understand. Not only that, but you are convinced that leaving for six weeks will allow problems to emerge that will take even longer to clean up. "Guys, that's nice of you, but really, I'm okay. Just a little tired is all."

Ed continues, "[You], hear my heart in this: We aren't asking you. We're telling you. Let's trust God for the details and figure it out. We care about you too much to not insist. We will work together to make sure everyone understands. Besides, we want you here for a long, long time."

The last statement seals it for you. You feel relieved and excited.

Disciplemaking Cultures Reflect Jesus

Disciplemaking cultures make disciples who look and act like Jesus. A disciplemaking culture transforms from the inside out. When Jesus is our model, our message, and our method, then people start trying to act like Jesus!

Healthy disciplemaking cultures transform individuals who are far removed from a leader's direct input. It happens just like Mark 4:27-29 describes:

> Night and day, whether he sleeps or gets up, the seed
> sprouts and grows, though he does not know how. All by
> itself the soil produces grain—first the stalk, then the head,
> then the full kernel in the head. As soon as the grain is ripe,
> he puts the sickle to it, because the harvest has come.

Jesus' aim wasn't simply to save a few, train them, and protect them from the world. It wasn't to gather thousands of followers, connect them to each other, and then serve them while they did good deeds in the world. No, His goals were to (1) invest in a few, train them, and then launch them into the world;[2] (2) develop a culture among the Twelve that was marked so deeply by surrender and mission that it would transform everything it touched; and (3) build a movement of disciplemakers who would change the world from then until eternity. And to the amazement of historians and social scientists, His methods worked!

A disciplemaking culture should be the goal within every local church and ministry because it was Jesus' goal. And He is our example.[3] In a disciplemaking culture people are influenced toward Jesus automatically, because a disciplemaking culture spins outward and permeates everything by propelling disciplemakers into every crevice of society—neighborhoods, workplaces, and associations, even crossing national boundaries.

This isn't hype. Jesus and His disciples proved it.

Church history is full of cultures that have had some or all of the ingredients of a disciplemaking culture in their DNA. Unfortunately, many of these cultures have faded away, while others have fallen victim to distraction, drift, neglect, and the tyranny of the urgent. We need to get back to the ways of Jesus, making disciplemakers and building cultures of disciplemaking that are centered on His example.

There is no greater leadership opportunity than culture building. In fact, the primary gift of leaders is the culture they cultivate and eventually pass on. If you believe that, then the need to be intentional in culture building is as great as the need to be intentional in disciplemaking. After all, building a disciplemaking culture starts with making disciples.

Can you imagine the difference a disciplemaking culture would make in your church, ministry, women's group, or small group? Can you envision the ripples such a culture could create? I trust you can. And I believe that you are hungry to build such a culture.

How Is a Disciplemaking Culture Built?

Now that we have a baseline understanding of disciplemaking, culture, and a disciplemaking culture, the remainder of this book will focus on how to construct *a durable foundation* for a disciplemaking culture.

Let's take a moment to acknowledge that when building anything in the Kingdom, there is only one foundation: Jesus Christ. Ephesians 2:20 specifically identifies Him as "the chief cornerstone," while the apostles and prophets form the rest of the foundation. The metaphor of Jesus as the foundation communicates the first principles upon which everything else is built. I use this metaphor to explain the beginning of a disciplemaking culture. It can get linguistically sticky to do so, but for the purposes of our exploration, Jesus is the very ground into which the disciplemaking foundation is laid. If it's built into anything else, it won't hold together. It's actually worse than that; Scripture tells us such a structure will be consumed by fire.[4]

Having established Jesus' rightful place, it's also important to recognize that disciplemaking cultures that endure are not built by a lone leader (despite the myths surrounding dynamic leadership), a program, or a curriculum. Simply stated, the foundation of a disciplemaking culture is a CORE team of disciplemakers.

A **CORE team** is a group of people who

have a Common vision,

Own that vision individually,

are Relationally resilient as a result of their connection to one
another and the mission, and

have the Endurance to weather discouragement, weariness,
and hardship in order to reach their objective.

The CORE team has two primary goals: (1) to become a team
and (2) for each person to become a disciplemaker. The purpose
in reaching those goals is so that the team can impact the greater
church/ministry culture. However, the ultimate purpose is to glorify God.

For many leaders, the concept of a team isn't new (although
CORE may be). But how such a team is developed isn't well
understood, illustrated, or practiced. Disciplemaking books and
resources tend to give an overview of the entire culture-building
process, but as important as it is to see the big picture, this can't
sufficiently guide a leader in building the foundation. Time and
again I've seen disciplemaking foundations rushed, neglected, or
completely ignored because the leaders thought casting the vision
was the work. Like Pisano (see chapter 1), these leaders may see
great momentum and "success" for the first few years, but their
work is soon doomed by the faulty foundation they laid.

Such a discovery often leads to discouraged leaders who want
to drop out of disciplemaking entirely. It's not that they are afraid
of the hard work of repair, but in their discouragement, they too
often turn instead to the next great idea. Foundation progress can't

be made until those leaders are refreshed in vision and equipped with tools to move forward in a new way.

Let me be clear, however: If you've discovered you have a faulty foundation, you can recover.

When a crooked-tower moment happens, the restoration work doesn't take place at the top of the tower; the task is to fix the foundation. When the goal is a disciplemaking culture, that involves working on the hearts of those who first laid that foundation.

The Foundation Makes the Difference

My assumption is that you are a leader who wants to build a disciplemaking culture in a church or ministry, but you aren't sure how to do it. What you are sure of is that the obstacles are clear and the task seems daunting. Perhaps others want things to remain the same. Maybe the existing culture is rooted in traditions and values that don't align with Jesus' style of disciplemaking. There may be some disciplemaking happening, but it's happening on the side, as opposed to being connected to the whole.

A disciplemaking culture can grow from any of these starting points. My goal is not to equip you to build an entire disciplemaking culture. Rather, what follows is intended to be the base upon which a more holistic disciplemaking strategy can be built.

Building a disciplemaking foundation that will stand the test of time isn't easy. Whether you want to build such a disciplemaking culture from scratch (for example, a church or ministry plant) or—as is more common—to repair, refurbish, or rehabilitate an existing culture, the process can be full of land mines and barriers. I know because I've developed disciplemaking foundations in different contexts as well as trained and coached many leaders as they developed other leaders. In each case, the foundation has made the difference between long-term sustainability and inevitable disappointment.

For now, remember the CORE team. It is the concrete and rebar upon which a disciplemaking culture is built. If there is no CORE team, there is little hope of a durable foundation.

In the next chapter, we'll look at why a CORE team is so important.

Reflection Questions

1. What's your reaction to culture not being *explicitly* mentioned in Scripture? Do you agree that it is still an important ministry focus? Why or why not?

2. How do you define *culture*? What's your reaction to the author's definition of culture as "the (mostly invisible) operating system" of a group?

3. Which of the disciplemaking portraits could you relate to most? Least? How did they impact your thinking about a disciplemaking culture?

4. What does the CORE acronym stand for? What element of the CORE team (common vision, individual ownership, relational resilience, endurance) is the most elusive for you as you try to develop a disciplemaking culture?

5. Communicate what you've discovered to God. What next step is He asking you to take?

THE CORE TEAM
AS THE FOUNDATION

The way a team plays as a whole determines its success. You may have the greatest bunch of individual stars in the world, but if they don't play together, the club won't be worth a dime.
BABE RUTH

I had been teaching in Thailand for just under a year when the assistant principal summoned me to his office.

That year was one of the most difficult years of my life. My wife, eight-month-old daughter, and I had condensed our possessions down to a couple of suitcases, said goodbye to family and friends, and moved to Thailand as missionaries. For twelve long months, we'd worked hard to learn the language, acculturate, and find ways to love and serve those around us. I expected the meeting to be related to my contract, but it turned out to be a conversation that I'll never forget.

"Most of the teachers think that you are selfish," the assistant principal said.

Ouch. I was stunned, and my internal translation services briefly went offline. I wondered, *How could he say that I'm selfish?* I had been diligent in learning Thai, regularly asked my co-teacher if she needed help with anything, spent downtime relating with other teachers, and had good rapport with the students and their parents. I thought everything was going well.

Somehow I recovered enough Thai vocabulary to ask why. My question was met with a question. "Well, have you asked the other teachers if they need help?"

"Yes, frequently," I replied, trying not to be defensive.

"No, no! Not just the teachers you teach with, but all the others?"

I was confused at this point. There were over sixty teachers in this large government school. I had yet to remember most of their names, let alone ask if they needed my help.

As our conversation continued, my boss told me I needed to go to every teacher in the school to ask how I could help them! I left his office frustrated, discouraged, and confused. My Thai friends at the school did their best to cheer me up, but in time, they gently revealed that they agreed with the assistant principal.

So I went around offering my help to the other teachers. Each one appreciated my offer. I was afraid I'd be inundated with requests I couldn't fulfill. Instead, not one of them asked me for anything.

I learned from all this that they saw me as selfish, not because I wasn't helping, but because most of the teachers didn't know they could count on me for help. From their perspective, I was engaging as an individual driven by my own priorities rather than as a team member who was ready to work with others for a greater team goal. In short, I wasn't being a good teammate.

This was my personal crooked-tower moment; it shook my confidence to the bone.

I'd joined the faculty as an American joins a group. I had my own reasons for being there (which of course included serving others). That day in the principal's office, however, I learned that I had joined something more cohesive and committed than a group of teachers. I'd joined a team.

The difference between a group and a team is significant. Groups come together around common interests for individual purposes and priorities. In other words, individuals join to get something that fits their own agenda. For example, one book club member may have joined to make friends, while another may want an external motivation to read more, and still another may want to fill time on Wednesday evenings. In groups, each individual defines the scope and purpose of his or her participation. The motivation determines the participation: The person seeking friendship may only read book summaries online to prepare for the discussion; the person who joined to read more may read each book cover to cover; the person seeking to fill time may read as much as he can between meetings. Without a unifying goal, the group may accomplish much, but it's unlikely that they will become a team.

Teams come together around a common vision or purpose, unlike groups that bring separate goals to their shared activities. A team exists to accomplish something that an individual or a group with separate goals cannot. Team members have individual motivations, but they are expected to put the team's goals ahead of their own. That shared agenda cultivates connection and interdependence that allows the team to reach their common goals.

As difficult as it was for me to hear, the assistant principal was right. I had behaved like a group member with a separate goal. My interaction with my teammates was selfish, not because I hadn't asked them if they needed help, but because I hadn't even considered that there was a common goal to work toward. That blind spot made me a bad teammate.

The Team as the Foundation

Many Americans struggle with being on a team, whether a large team like I was on in Thailand or a small team at a church or in a neighborhood association. With some exceptions (notably sports and sometimes family), American culture is individualistic. It's been passed down through historical narratives that glorify independence and individualism. We are a nation of do-it-yourselfers; we are encouraged to look out for number one. Sure, we use the word *team* at work or at church, but most of us find the comfort of personal control that groups offer preferable to the demands of teams.

A CORE group can't build an effective foundation. A foundation requires a CORE *team*.

The CORE team not only supports the weight of disciplemaking in a culture, but it also spurs on the momentum of disciplemaking. In order for disciplemaking cultures to emerge, there must be leaders and models for others to emulate. The CORE team provides leaders and models of disciplemaking.

Conversely, if disciplemaking develops without a CORE team, progress will eventually sink, crack, and crumble under the weight of disciplemaking ministry just like the Leaning Tower of Pisa.

It's heartbreaking to witness disciplemaking implode after years of hard-fought growth. I'm not saying the effort was wasted, just that it didn't develop into a culture of disciplemaking. Without a CORE team, no lasting disciplemaking culture will emerge. It really is that simple.

Jesus' Example

Jesus and Paul developed teams in order to build a disciplemaking foundation. Since Jesus' way of making disciples is the best way and our ultimate example, let's start by looking at what He did.

During the first year of His public ministry, Jesus invested deeply in five disciples: Andrew, Peter, Philip, Nathanael, and John.[1] There is a lot we don't know about this year, but many scholars agree that it wasn't until after this first year that Jesus called the Twelve to follow Him in a new way.[2]

Jesus' plan for His team is shown in passages like Mark 3:14-15 ("He appointed twelve that they might be with him and that he might send them out to preach and to have authority to drive out demons") and Acts 1:8 ("'But you will receive power when the Holy Spirit comes on you; and you will be my witnesses in Jerusalem, and in all Judea and Samaria, and to the ends of the earth'"). The Gospels show close relationships among the disciples that included arguments, struggle, and interdependence. They fought like brothers over who was greatest, they were sent out two by two as ministry partners, and they failed together in the Garden of Gethsemane.

Jesus had a team, but He also had an individual relationship with each disciple on the team. The training happened at both the team level and the individual level. The connection point between the two is Jesus' presence. Surely on their daylong walks, mountain retreats, and ministry experiences Jesus ministered to them at times individually, in pairs, in triads, and so on. In fact, we see these interactions in the Gospels when He addresses Peter in Luke 22:31-34; James and John in Mark 10:35-40; and Peter, James, and John together in Matthew 17:1-13. This dual focus on the team and the individual allowed Him to form the disciples into a team whose culture carried a disciplemaking DNA that would one day reach the rest of the world.

Paul's Example

Paul employed a similar team strategy when he planted disciplemaking churches. In Thessalonica, the team began with just three: Paul, Silas, and Timothy.[3] As a team, they lived with the Thessalonians and modeled for them what a disciple's life looked like. Upon that small yet powerful foundation, some of the locals took notice and began to imitate them. As the number of disciples increased, others started to become like those disciples. As the spiritual generations flowed outward, they became a "model to all the believers in Macedonia and Achaia." And soon after, "the Lord's message rang out from you not only in Macedonia and Achaia—your faith in God has become known everywhere."[4]

A close reading of the Pauline Epistles shows that Paul repeated this team strategy over and over again. He left behind teams of disciples to lead those disciplemaking churches. For example, not only did Paul remind the Ephesians of their different leadership roles,[5] but he also ended most of his letters by individually greeting the leaders. For Paul, church leadership was a *we* thing, not a *me* thing. Paul identified and developed CORE team leadership that served as the foundation of the disciplemaking culture in each church he helped establish.

Leading Change

The team approach that Jesus and Paul employed to change individuals and culture is compelling. Unfortunately, outside the directive to follow the example of Jesus, the Bible doesn't offer a comprehensive explanation about how to shift a culture from one thing to another. Is the CORE team approach really essential to the process?

John Kotter, the Konosuke Matsushita Professor of Leadership, Emeritus, at Harvard University, is known as the authority on leadership and culture change.[6] In 2011, *Time* magazine selected his book *Leading Change* as one of the twenty-five most influential business management books ever written.[7] For decades now, Kotter's insight into culture change has proved helpful and effective in thousands of contexts all over the world. And his process just so happens to pair well with Jesus' model.

Kotter writes convincingly about the consequences of undervaluing a team approach (which he also calls a *guiding coalition*) to cultural transformation:

> Efforts that lack a sufficiently powerful *guiding coalition*
> can make apparent progress for a while. The organizational
> structure might be changed, or a reengineering effort might
> be launched. But sooner or later, countervailing forces
> undermine the initiatives.[8]

Later he drives home the point:

> Because major change is so difficult to accomplish,
> a powerful force is required to sustain the process. No
> one individual, not even a monarch-like CEO, is ever
> able to develop the right vision, communicate it to
> large numbers of people, eliminate all the key obstacles,
> generate short-term wins, lead and manage dozens of
> change projects, and anchor new approaches deep in the
> organization's culture. Weak committees are even worse.
> A strong guiding coalition is always needed—one with
> the right composition, level of trust, and shared objective.
> *Building such a team is always an essential part* of the early
> stages of any effort to restructure, reengineer, or retool a
> set of strategies.[9]

Whether knowingly or not, Kotter has given language to the principles Jesus used in building the most powerful disciplemaking team the world has ever known. The message of the gospel continues to emanate from Jesus' CORE team to the ends of the earth, from age to age.

Throughout the book, I will continue to reference Jesus' example and principles, as well as Kotter's seeming affirmation of those principles. I want there to be no mistake about the power of a disciplemaking foundation built with a CORE team to enact cultural change. The fact that Jesus' principles can be discovered by Kotter and others confirms their effectiveness and affirms their ability to adapt to different contexts.

Unfortunately, not just anyone can build a CORE team. In the next chapter, I will explain why a CORE team of disciplemakers must be led by a disciplemaker.

Reflection Questions

1. What is the difference between a team and a group?

2. Why is a group insufficient to lay a disciplemaking foundation?

3. In what ways is it easier to lead a group than it is to lead a CORE team?

4. Are you convinced that a CORE team is essential for culture change? Why or why not?

5. Communicate what you've discovered to God. What next step is He asking you to take?

DISCIPLEMAKER AS LEAD BUILDER

You can't teach what you don't know; you can't lead where you don't go.
REV. JESSE JACKSON

Sculptors don't have the same knowledge as architects. Sculptors wouldn't necessarily have understood what architects knew, namely that building a tower in Pisa was a very challenging task! *Pisa* literally means "marshy land." The soil beneath the city was a soft mixture of sand, silt, and clay—much too unstable to support a tower. Foundations are important everywhere, but this was especially true for building in Pisa.

Despite the challenges, experts have concluded that a different foundation would have eliminated the problem altogether.[1] Bonanno Pisano didn't know better since he wasn't an architect; he was an artist, a showman. He couldn't really think like an architect.

How do I know Bonanno was a showman? Archaeologists dug

up a stone from the base of the tower about 650 years after construction began. The stone reads, *I, who without doubt have erected this marvellous work that is above all others, am the citizen of Pisa by the name of Bonanno.*[2] Scholars believe the stone sat at the foot of the tower as Pisano worked on it. Once the lean was discovered, an embarrassed Pisano returned to the tower to bury the stone.[3]

Instead of rising to the level of his vision, Bonanno fell to the level of his training. He learned that laying an adequate and lasting foundation requires the mind and skill of an architect.

In the same way, a lasting disciplemaking foundation can only be built with the mindset and skill of a disciplemaker. It sounds obvious, doesn't it? Unfortunately, it's not. Every year, Christian leaders believe they can build an entire culture of multiplying disciples without ever having engaged in disciplemaking in a serious, intentional way. Their results are similar to Bonanno's—a few years of apparent success followed by unforeseen problems they don't know how to solve. Such attempts often leave their ministries worse off than they were before. After all, it's easier to build a foundation from scratch than it is to repair a faulty one.

Is this disheartening? The point isn't to discourage those who have already attempted to lay or fix a disciplemaking foundation, but rather to encourage careful consideration in those who are about to try.

Unlike Bonanno, most Christian leaders aren't motivated by their own glory. In fact, most begin building a disciplemaking culture in response to a lean they have already discovered in their ministry culture. Whether that lean is an inward-facing culture, a culture that lacks others-first service, or even a culture that is relationally sharp toward one another, motivation matters. Simply put, *why* a leader decides to build a disciplemaking culture determines *how* that leader will build that culture. Those who lack a biblically rooted disciplemaking paradigm are most often motivated to build a disciplemaking culture for one of four reasons.

Four Common Motivations for Building a Culture and the Problems They Create

Before we look at these common motivations, I want to emphasize that the purpose isn't to critique the church/ministry models represented; it's to highlight the ways your motivation will impact how your culture ends up being built. Taking the time to reflect on your motivation will help you adjust and build more skillfully.

1. Survival

The first common motivation is *survival*. Ministries all across America have found themselves in a slow decline for years now. More and more Americans are choosing to avoid church altogether. The decline in church involvement was 7 percent between 2009 and 2019.[4] Post-pandemic statistics indicate that while the decline has slowed,[5] it certainly hasn't stopped.[6] Combine this decline with the reality that many churches need to bring in around 32 percent more new members in a given year just to counteract attrition, and revitalization becomes very difficult.[7] Church growth experts recommend small groups, community engagement, leadership development, and discipleship programs. To the ears of many desperate leaders, a disciplemaking culture sounds like a combination of all the above.

A ministry leader who looks to disciplemaking to survive faces a *problem of priority*. Pursuing a disciplemaking culture in order to gain members is dangerous because there's a significant qualitative difference between a church member and a disciple. The emphasis on church membership can be traced back to the fourth century, when participation in Christianity was strongly incentivized through legislation by the Roman government.[8] The shift for the church was large and lasting. Instead of a place to come and die, the church became a club to join and enjoy. Within the club, social status and prestige were up for grabs. Pews were purchased like seats at a stadium with the best going to those willing to pay the most. The show happened on Sunday mornings, and the chief obligation of members was to attend and give.

In a culture that highly values assembling masses, the membership model is a good fit. Pastors are often evaluated by counting butts, baptisms, and bread ($). When the numbers are favorable, pastors are patted on the back and rewarded with raises and opportunities at larger venues. On the other side, parishioners get to count without paying the price that the cross demands. By being faithful members, the spiritually immature end up in places of honor and leadership in the church community. In other words, *it's a win-win: The people get religion without obligation, and the leaders get to lead without the hassle of loving like Jesus did.*

The primary problem of the membership model is the culture it creates. When the goal is masses, not maturity, the church develops an unhealthy, ingrown culture. Let me explain.

In a membership culture, the force is centripetal; it pulls inward. A clear distinction is made between those who are in and those who are out. The initial call to a nonmember is to join. The continuing call of a member is to contribute. The types of individuals the culture celebrates is telling. In a membership culture, those who attend the most, give the most (money and/or time), and persuade the most nonmembers to become members are the ones who are celebrated. **Since members are drawn inward, they expect that those they seek to reach *will come to* the organization.** In this way, the organization intentionally sustains and grows itself by making new members.

By contrast, a disciplemaking culture initially draws people inward, but only for the purpose of propelling them outward. The inward movement develops the disciple for deployment outside the organization. The initial call of a nondisciple is to follow. The continuing call of a disciple is to follow and bear fruit. Again, the types of individuals the culture celebrates is telling. In a disciplemaking culture, individuals who follow and bear fruit *in the context of the lost* (regardless of whether or not those reached ever join the culture) are the ones who are celebrated. **Since the disciples are moving outward, they expect to go to those they seek to reach.** As they go, the organization intentionally grows the Kingdom and fulfills Jesus' command to make disciples of all nations.

C. S. Lewis said, "The Church exists for nothing else but to draw men into Christ, to make them little Christs. If they are not doing that, all the cathedrals, clergy, missions, sermons, even the Bible itself, are simply a waste of time. God became man for no other purpose."[9]

Pastors and churches must be evaluated based on the kind of disciple they send out into the world. Each and every Christian is called to be a disciple and to make disciples. There is no exception.

It takes longer to grow disciplemakers than it does to grow members. Member-focused disciplemaking can become rushed for the sake of numbers. But it also bends toward organizational needs rather than the needs of the individual. The problem isn't having members; it's that members aren't being made into disciples.

In other words, there's no need for a dichotomy when it comes to members and disciples. However, which takes *primary importance*—the individual disciple or the organization—remains a crucial aspect of how the disciplemaking unfolds. Jesus' style of disciplemaking is never primarily about filling an organizational need. Individuals must know they are being engaged from a place of love and from a desire to help them grow to maturity in Christ— in every sense—not merely to help the church or ministry survive.

2. Attraction

The second common motivation is *attraction*. The root of this motivation is similar to the first—a need for more people. The problem most attractional ministries share is the "back door"— people who had been engaged wind up leaving. But the landscape of church engagement makes it harder and harder to attract new individuals. So the response from attractional churches is to constantly work to offer *the* best worship experience, *the most* engaging preaching, and *the most* innovative and interesting programming.

Instead of being in danger of closing their doors, attractional ministries are fighting one of two battles: either to keep growing numerically or to keep their staff and building. Staff and building expenses are significant. One analysis of five hundred churches found that staff salaries are about 50 percent of the typical budget, with some as high as 70 percent.[10] Combine that with an average of 22 percent of the budget spent on facilities,[11] and you can see why I've found these church leaders so burdened to attract people.[12]

When attendance dips, so does giving. This leads many to adopt numeric growth as their primary metric of health. Building a disciplemaking culture might be attractive to these churches because it appears to close the back door by growing people who can be sent out to invite others in.

Those motivated primarily by attraction face *a problem of scale*. Attractional churches thrive on lots of events that can touch everyone (themed Sunday services, community engagement events, etc.). These events are planned by staff leadership and are designed to be executed by willing but unskilled volunteers. Disciplemaking, by contrast, is a slow-to-unfold process that takes years to impact the whole culture. It doesn't take place on an events timetable.

Leaders of attractional ministries often go to great lengths to speed up the process of building a disciplemaking culture. They may create a curriculum that subdivides the disciplemaking process into bite-size elements, hold short and narrowly focused training classes, and then simply turn the willing loose to go "disciple" anyone who is interested. (By which I mean taking them through the curriculum.) Such efforts, though well intended, flood the culture with individuals whose view of disciplemaking is overly structured and formulaic—"spiritual mentoring" that lacks the vitality, vision, and ability to impact generations. Worse yet, those narrow views of what constitutes discipleship are what get reproduced in others.

3. Spiritual Growth

A third common motivation leaders have in building a disciplemaking culture is to *grow spiritual leaders*. Typically, these ministries are stable, but they face the challenge of replacing aging leaders. For years, they've had trouble developing younger leaders, but the bigger problem is getting older leaders to invest in younger ones. A generational component is at work here. Though Gen Z Christians are the most interested generation in disciplemaking (with millennials not far behind), Christian Boomers are the least interested in it.[13] For these ministries, disciplemaking is a way to move older leaders to invest in and raise up the next generation of leadership.

The problem that accompanies this motivation is *a problem of vision.* The strategy of helping older spiritual leaders invest in younger leaders is often successful in the short term. But unless the older leaders model an outward ministry mindset (often lacking from the outset), the result of this disciplemaking motivation ends where it began—with new spiritual leaders who lack vision for the greater mission. Leadership and discipleship are two different things. A spiritual leader is not necessarily the same as a disciple-maker. Jesus engaged the Twelve primarily as an act of obedience to God[14] and, secondarily, to grow "fishers of men,"[15] not to raise up religious leaders who would provide organizational leadership.

Jesus' way of training and development bears witness to His outward mindset. He came for those who were sick, not those who were healthy;[16] He appointed them to be with Him so that He could send them out to preach and "to drive out demons";[17] and He left them the mission of making "disciples of all nations."[18] Each step of their training moved them outward, not inward.

Working toward a disciplemaking culture to develop spiritual leaders puts the cart before the horse. The engine of a disciplemaking culture is its outward movement to the oppressed, the addicted, and those separated from Christ. Disciplemaking is for everyone, not just those with the spiritual gift of leadership. Churches who leverage disciplemaking to raise up spiritual leaders risk developing a caste system within the church. Instead of disciplemaking being seen as for everyone, it becomes known as something for "superstar" Christians only, causing everyday disciples to feel left out. Jesus looked for the spiritually hungry, not the spiritually healthy.[19]

4. Missional

The fourth motivation is *missional.* As church attendance declines, many Christian leaders realize the need to move out into the culture—a good aim. Not only has attendance been in decline, but so has the degree to which Americans use the Bible. Since Scripture is central to the life of Christ-followers, a decline in Bible engagement is arguably a better indicator of faith than church attendance (especially since church attendance was disrupted during the pandemic). In the two years following COVID, those who used the Bible (who read, listened to, or prayed with the Bible on their own, outside a church service or church event) three or more times in the past year fell from 50 percent (where it had been for about a decade) to 39 percent.[20] As the population of engaged disciples declines, the growing unreached population grows. Leaders who observe these two realities often see a disciplemaking culture as a way to equip people to be sent out on missional initiatives.

The problem of a missional motivation is *a problem of love.* To be clear, it doesn't have to be this way, but frequently, when evangelistic motivation drives disciplemaking, it narrows the gospel and distorts the church's responsibility to grow immature disciples to maturity. Put another way, if leaders are too focused on reaching the lost, they run the risk of neglecting those they are called to serve.[21] Instead of loving others within their own relational network, people settle for serving people far removed from their context. Programmatic, nonrelational ministry allows individuals to serve others without loving them. Serving others in program-driven, nonrelational ways such as packaging holiday boxes, distributing meals, or providing space for a basketball league depersonalizes the serving and the served. It does so by providing a picture of ministry that is completely separated from the spiritual giftings of those serving and from an appreciation of the complex needs of those being served. Such nonrelational ministries aren't wrong, but they aren't Jesus-style disciplemaking. In fact, the Scriptures hold no examples of this kind of relationally disconnected serving. Instead of inspiring these young servants to mature so that they can help others know Christ and grow to maturity as well, they enable the illusion of Christlike love without the sacrifice that Christlike love demands. Disciplemaking requires more. Disciplemaking requires people to know and love those they are serving.

Each of these motivations springs from the genuine desire people have to do the best they can with the training they have received. Christian leaders rightly desire to reach the unreached and to build churches or ministries, but these motivations alone will not lead to a lasting disciplemaking culture. This means that whatever disciplemaking impact they have will have a lean to it.

Fruitful Disciplemaking Motivations

What motivations provide fertile ground to grow a disciplemaking culture? And who needs to lead the work of disciplemaking in order for a disciplemaking culture to emerge? There are at least three motivations.

1. The first fruitful motivation is *Christological*—a desire to be like Jesus in character and in action. A person with a Christological motivation engages disciplemaking because Jesus did, and they want to be like Him. It's not enough to be moral, to faithfully shepherd the sheep, to raise a family, or to serve others. No, these disciplemakers are motivated to become just like Jesus. Since Jesus' life is their example, disciplemaking is central to their calling. It's not something they do; it's who they are becoming. Such deeply motivated commitment isn't simple obedience;[22] it's their very life— their way of being in the world.

   This motivation leads them to actually believe that they are called to do even greater things than Jesus did.[23] For such disciplemakers, it's not enough to make a couple of disciples. Instead, they are aiming for a team of disciples who will have the faith to challenge and change the world. They want to trust God that such a team will spark a movement of disciplemakers.

2. The second fruitful motivation is *a Kingdom motivation*— a desire to expand the Kingdom by saving those who don't yet know Jesus. Those who carry this motivation are strongly compelled by the idea of depopulating hell and reaching all nations. They are compelled to play a part in building an eternal Kingdom where every tribe, tongue, language, and people gathers together around the throne to worship the King.[24]

3. The third fruitful motivation is *generational*—a desire to participate in the covenantal promises God gave in Genesis. These disciplemakers are convinced that the covenantal promise[25] that God gave Abraham, Isaac, and Jacob—to make their offspring as numerous as the stars in the sky—is available to them as well.[26] They have seen how that promise was passed down from the Old Testament into the New Testament. They embrace their life as a thin span of time and want to use it to build the Kingdom. They desire to serve the purposes God has for them in this generation.[27] They believe they've been invited to partner with God to do something that holds meaning in this life and in eternity. Such a generational motivation allows these disciplemakers to mine the Scriptures for the promises made to others and to ask God to do the same in their lives. Here are some examples:

- Isaiah 43:4: [God says,] "Since you are precious and honored in my sight, and because I love you, I will give people in exchange for you, nations in exchange for your life."

- Isaiah 60:22: "The least of you will become a thousand, the smallest a mighty nation. I am the LORD; in its time I will do this swiftly."

- Galatians 3:29: "If you belong to Christ, then you are Abraham's seed, and heirs according to the promise."

Generationally motivated disciplemakers read passages like these and cry out, *God, would You do this in my life?*

They understand they have a part to play in the grand unfolding of God's story as He builds His Kingdom— a people set apart for Himself. God uses ordinary, everyday people to do this. As Christ's disciples, they have a great spiritual heritage[28] that motivates them in disciplemaking.

Virtually every fruitful disciplemaker is motivated by one or more of these three primary motivations. Each motivation is rooted in what God desires yet also connects to the heart of the individual disciplemaker. The result is a disciplemaker who has both intrinsic and extrinsic motivation.

No matter how a disciplemaker is motivated, Scripture is clear that God wants to use every disciple to build the church by advancing the gospel and establishing His Kingdom on earth.[29] His plan hinges on using every disciple to build the church by making disciplemakers. These humble disciplemakers not only have a great spiritual heritage, but they are also being cheered on by a great cloud of witnesses in the heavenly realms![30]

Let's not overcomplicate this. Disciplemaking should be led by a disciplemaking team. In the absence of a team, it must be led by a disciplemaker. Either way, the work is spread by those who are passionate enough to light a fire in others. Disciplemaking cannot be led by someone who has never made a disciplemaker. It sounds obvious, right?

Yet every year, pastors or church leaders are asked to make a disciplemaking culture or a disciplemaking team when they've never made even one disciplemaker. It just doesn't work that way.

What's Your Motivation?

Christian leaders who make disciples are committed to building up the body of Christ by bringing the faithful to maturity and by bringing skeptics to Christ. Such commitment to living like Jesus is costly. Disciplemaking leaders, especially pastors, are often attacked by their own. For example, Ryan, a pastor friend of mine, was told by his leadership team that he needed to stop spending time discipling individuals. Although Ryan had decades of experience pastoring, he was new to the church and quickly learned how they viewed disciplemaking. They boldly asked him to champion disciplemaking but to avoid spending time *doing* it. Instead, according to Ryan, they wanted him to focus on "preaching and the business of the church."

It's not that the leadership team was uninterested in disciplemaking; their motivation was split, however, between attraction and survival. The church wanted Ryan to preach amazing sermons and to run more programs with the hope that others would be attracted to the church. For them, church progress was measured more by masses than multipliers, by observers of the mission more than doers of the mission.

Many churches unknowingly pit their picture of ministry against disciplemaking. For Jesus there was no division in the mission. Jesus' care for every individual led Him to act. He was moved to act by healing Bartimaeus on the road to Jericho,[31] driving out the demons from the demoniac in the region of the Gerasenes,[32] and healing the paralytic in Capernaum.[33] Jesus didn't just see masses, He also saw faces. It was that sight that drove him to tears as He looked at the crowds in each town, village, and synagogue. Matthew 9 tells us that Jesus' tears were because people were "harassed and helpless, like sheep without a shepherd." The solution to this problem wasn't preaching or programmed care ministry, the solution was more workers. His strategy was twofold: prayer and making disciples who become disciplemakers.[34]

Jesus-style disciplemaking is not opposed to preaching or to the "business of the church" (as though making disciples were something other than the church's business). Quite the contrary, Jesus invested significant time preaching and caring for the crowds—sometimes for days at a time. He did those things out of His deep care for them, not out of obligation.[35] He met their physical needs while also developing more shepherds and shepherd-makers who could fully meet their ongoing spiritual needs.

Christian leaders who care for the masses like Jesus did will engage disciplemaking as the long-term strategy to reach the masses. Preaching and pastoral care were never the main focus of Jesus' ministry, but they complemented His main mission of making disciples.[36]

Pastor Ryan's leadership team asked him to do something that contradicted the example of Jesus. Rather than compromise on disciplemaking, Ryan left. As a disciplemaker, his priority is to make disciples. Disciplemakers *make disciples*. It's more than a priority; it's *the* priority. No. Matter. What.

What's your motivation for building a disciplemaking culture? If you've already started building one, how has your motivation impacted your actions? If your pastor or ministry leader isn't a disciplemaker, please don't expect him to lay a disciplemaking foundation. If he's trying to lead disciplemaking before he's lived it, consider what might be motivating him and what lean might result. Regardless, don't expect him to lay the foundation before he's made a disciple. Only a disciplemaker can lay a disciple-making foundation. And only a disciplemaker can effectively lead a disciplemaking culture.

For some leaders, that's a sobering reality. I've met many who have faithfully led churches for decades but have never made a reproducing disciple. Frequently, it's not their fault. They have done what they were trained to do. They know that the purpose of the church is to make disciples, but they have never been taught how to do it. Most graduated from seminary without a single class on how to make a disciple. Instead, they were trained in guarding sound doctrine, faithfully preaching the Word, and shepherding people through the journey of life. These are good, biblical things, but they aren't sufficient—in and of themselves—to make healthy disciplemakers.

If you are a disciplemaker—even a young one—you are ready to learn how to create a disciplemaking culture, not just make individual disciples. Every disciplemaking movement starts with disciplemakers. Are you willing for God to use you to start the movement at your church? Though movements begin with one person, you can't do it alone. A vision can only be fulfilled by partnering with others. Partnership is vital, and as discussed in chapter 3, developing a CORE team is the foundation that will support generations of disciplemakers.

Being the Change You Wish to See

How something is done makes a big difference in the impact of that action. A sense of urgency is key to catalyzing change.[37]

Kotter says, "By far the biggest mistake people make when trying to change organizations is to plunge ahead without establishing a high enough sense of urgency. . . . Transformations always fail to achieve their objectives when complacency levels are high."[38]

To establish urgency, the leader must lead. You must be out front, being the change you wish to see. "Leadership is about vision," Kotter writes, "about people buying in, about empowerment and, most of all, about producing useful change. Leadership is not about attributes, it's about behavior."[39] In other words, urgency is deeper than getting people to do something; it grows out of buying into the motivation. The *why* changes the *how*.

J. Stewart Black, another organizational change expert, puts it this way:

> Lasting success comes from changing individuals first . . . because organizations change only as far or as fast as their collective individuals change. . . . Sometimes, changing individuals means changing yourself as the starting point.[40]

Research and experience show that the key to changing culture isn't changing programs, it's changing people. You must help one before you help many. And once you have one, you need to develop another, and then finally you can develop a team.

Developing a CORE Team

To the disciplemaking leader, the CORE team is like a raised garden box where he tries to grow the kind of disciplemaking culture he desires to see in the field of the whole ministry. If he can't do it in the relatively small and uncomplicated garden box, he has little chance of being successful in the whole field.

The first part of developing a CORE team is cultivating a common vision. Vision isn't new to churches, businesses, or other organizations. Many churches spend significant time developing statements they hope will impact the behavior of the people. Typically, leaders are perplexed at the apathetic response from the people. The problem isn't one of hearing—it's one of seeing. Getting team members to see something new is the first challenge a CORE team must face. When a CORE team develops a common vision, they can move forward in their mission. Without a common vision, the team will lack the direction and confidence to carry out what they have been called to do. We will discuss this in the next chapter.

Reflection Questions

1. Are you a disciplemaker? What "Timothy" would identify you as their "Paul"?

2. Write one paragraph on why you want to lay a disciplemaking foundation.

3. Are you willing to build a disciplemaking foundation even if it causes your church's attendance and giving to fall (but still makes multiplying disciples)?

4. What other disciplemakers come to mind in your church who could help you establish a disciplemaking foundation?

5. Communicate what you've discovered to God. What next step is He asking you to take?

COMMON VISION

If you want to build a ship, don't drum up people to collect wood and don't assign them tasks and work, but rather teach them to long for the endless immensity of the sea.
ATTRIBUTED TO ANTOINE DE SAINT-EXUPÉRY

Did you know that for over two hundred years people believed that California was an island?[1] It happened innocently enough. In the early sixteenth century, Hernán Cortés was exploring the western coast of North America and, upon landing at what is now Baja California, reported having discovered an idyllic island. Only later, after excursions up the Gulf of California for hundreds of miles, with land on both sides and a horizon of water ahead and behind, was it discovered that Cortés had landed on a peninsula, not an island.[2]

The belief that California was an island endured, however, reinforced by later, inadequately equipped expeditions.[3] Maps were printed, people were educated, and the flawed assumption became the assumed reality.[4] Accepting California as an island was commonplace for two hundred years.[5]

Bad maps cause major problems—especially when someone tries to introduce a better map. Skepticism is understandable, though. People trust the map they have, and what it tells them becomes the lens through which all new data is interpreted. The old map, however inaccurate, has become *the way*.

Maps of the Church

In the West, most believers have carried the same discipleship map for generations. In the pursuit of spiritual maturity, attendance and knowledge retention have been the primary metrics. Most modern churches have offered a brand of Christianity that separates belief from obedience and salvation from discipleship. Separating the two leads everyday Christians to believe that growing to maturity and reproducing through disciplemaking are optional parts of following Jesus.

It's helpful to remember that cultivating a CORE team is how you will introduce the new map into the church culture. In this way, you can reestablish a holistic view of what it means to be a disciple—a vision that unites beliefs with obedience and obedience with transformation over time. The process is slow and requires helping people unlearn untruths in order to embrace eternal truths. When a disciplemaking culture is the goal, steering people toward the fruitful motivations and helping them connect the dots within the context of disciplemaking are the means.

When Jesus-style disciplemaking is presented to your CORE team, some members will internally struggle with what they hear as a redefinition of the "gospel deal" they accepted. They may believe that there is no need to engage in Jesus' mission because they've been saved by grace alone. This belief has led many to inaction. Author and theologian Dallas Willard once said, "We have not only been saved by grace, we have been paralyzed by it."[6] Disciplemaking is NOT about earning salvation, but as James asserts, we cannot separate belief from action.[7] Even Luther stated that idle faith doesn't justify.[8] At the very least, leaders need to be aware of this common inner struggle. There's much more that could be said on this, but I will close this can of worms by referring interested readers to two excellent books by Bill Hull that dive deeply into this important discussion.[9]

The old discipleship map grows disciples through classes and theological education. Those who show aptitude in learning become teachers. Everyone else is asked to attend services and serve where they can. This discipleship map is deeply etched into the mind of each church member.

With this map, the result is predictable: more conversations, followed by little action and even less accountability. This well-established pattern has implicitly trained church members that their part in discipleship is to learn and to passively support leadership. Jesus-style disciplemaking has simply never been a part of their map!

Regardless of how clearly a new disciplemaking vision is articulated, many committed Christians struggle to accept their personal responsibility in disciplemaking. They are used to nodding in agreement as a leader's vision is articulated. They are used to talking about how the church can become more relational, more effective in its outreach, and more focused on helping believers grow. They are, far too often, not used to doing anything about it.

To make a difference, the new map must lead the disciple to act differently. Successful team leaders must take the time to define terms, confront errors, and model the desired culture. This process is time consuming and sometimes painful. Remember, it takes time for people to let go of an old map and trust a new one.

Disciplemaking Maps and Vision

Conceptually, developing a new map is the same as clarifying a vision. Organizational leaders spend long hours crafting vision statements that are unveiled with great pomp. Over and over again, these vision statements are received with a polite golf clap and then promptly forgotten until leaders redo it a few years later.

Why do so many vision statements fall flat?

A statement is meant to be understood. A map is meant to be lived into. A vision statement falls flat because it goes nowhere. By contrast, a map has an impact because it points people somewhere.

Effective disciplemaking maps connect everyday life with God's eternal purposes. They are God-sized—formed with an understanding of who God is, what God is doing, and how He's designed us to join Him in that work. They invite everyday disciples to connect their individual growth to the lost all throughout the world. A God-sized vision forces us to struggle with how we're going to accomplish it. It demands the involvement of the whole community—each individual—because the task is so great. God has called us to reach the nations from where we are. So how do you reach the nations from your neighborhood? God intends for us to struggle with this question because He designed the answer to fit us like a glove.

As an adolescent, I struggled with the futility of life. Go to school, get a job, work for fifty years, retire, and die. And for what? In a hundred years, no one will even know my name. I longed to be part of something bigger than myself. I wanted to do something that would outlast me in the world.

I'm not alone in this—God has placed eternity in your heart as well.[10] In His sovereignty God has wired the same longings in the heart of every human. They may be expressed in various ways, but every human deeply longs to be loved, to be wanted, to be needed to accomplish something important, and to be part of something that will outlast their life.

God not only created us with these longings, but He also designed our role in the Kingdom to fulfill these longings. God's invitation into Kingdom work is as much about helping us thrive as it is about helping others. The call to make disciples of all nations is intended to fulfill our desires more fully than anything the world can offer. When disciples turn away from their Kingdom calling, they walk into a life of diminished connection and fulfillment.

The vision of disciplemaking began to take root in me at age twenty-one thanks to a well-timed question. My discipler said: "Most things on the earth will eventually pass away, but not everything. What can you see on the earth that will also be in eternity?" At the time, I wasn't sure. The answer? People and the Word of God.

Like a growing thirst on a hot summer day, that question grew from a thought to a yearning. I wanted to give myself to something that would outlast my life—something with eternal ramifications. Investing my life in others was the obvious and biblical way to do that.

Disciplemaking cultures have a pulse that is passed from one person to another. Don't get me wrong, the vision should still be *heard in large group settings*, but it's *felt in smaller settings of five or less*. By contrast, when a God-sized vision is primarily communicated in big groups, it's rarely received by the heart's antenna.

The Challenge of Drawing a New Map

The leader must be prepared for friction that follows challenging the old map. The confrontation between the old map and the new map is a necessary part of the process. As disciplemaking expert Bill Hull said, "There are no converts without confrontation."[11] This friction is actually a positive indication: Team members have little chance of truly seeing the new map unless it has been effectively distinguished from the old one.

CORE team leaders can engage negative reactions with humility and compassion. It takes courage to lead this way and to continue pressing into the discussion with clarity, understanding, and strength as opposed to shelving the conversation or minimizing the differences in maps. Leaders can lean into the relationship as team members struggle (more about that in chapter 6). Remember, many Christians have already been on a journey, and now they are seeing that the map they've been following isn't what they thought! It's natural for them to respond with some negativity. These reactions can be a challenge for the team leader—especially if team members are uncomfortable with conflict.

Pastor Colin faced this challenge early on in the team-building process when he contrasted the old map with the new one. Mike, thirty years Colin's senior, had trouble grasping the new map.

Recognizing Mike's struggle, Colin intentionally engaged with him after team meetings, patiently addressing his concerns and answering his questions. Later, he invited Mike to lunch to build the relational connection and to create space for dialogue. After a few months, Mike began to see the differences between the old and the new map—which brought up an even bigger problem for him.

Colin noticed Mike was withdrawing from the team discussions. Suspecting he was still skeptical, Colin arranged a meetup at the local coffee shop. They chatted a bit before shifting the conversation to disciplemaking. As they did, Mike's whole demeanor changed. He looked at Colin and said, "I think I understand what you are trying to get our team to do. And I can see the good in it." His words came out slow and purposeful, but Mike paused here, and Colin saw the tears in his eyes.

Mike composed himself and continued. "But are you saying I haven't made any disciples in my life?" Mike, who was nearly seventy-five, was a gentle and faithful man who had been a pillar of the church for decades.

Colin quickly responded, "No, absolutely not. God asks us to be faithful and obedient, and you have! I don't know the impact of your past ministry. But I do know that God has been honored and pleased by your faithfulness. That's what He wants from us. He wants us to faithfully obey what He shows us. This team and this process is about continuing in your faithfulness and increasing your fruitfulness. Just as you have been faithful to what He has shown you in the past, I am confident you will be faithful to what He's showing you now."

Mike softened and smiled slightly. "Well, I suppose I can do that."

Jesus' Example

Mike's struggle isn't unusual. Older disciples sometimes struggle with their past when they see the difference between the old map and the new map. Other team members may react strongly when they grasp that they are expected to personally disciple others. Their reactions can vary widely, from humble willingness to hostile defensiveness—such as saying the staff is trying to get everyone else to do the work they should be doing!

Jesus worked through the same sort of map problem with His team. In the Gospels we see Him repeatedly preaching about the new map ("You have heard that it was said. . . . But I tell you"), teaching about the new map ("Whoever wants to be my disciple must deny themselves and take up their cross daily and follow me"),[12] and modeling the new map ("Lord, are you going to wash my feet?"[13]). Jesus understood that if He wanted people to do something different, they would need to be taught something different. A fun study to do is to read the Gospels looking for the *new* map that Jesus helped His team see.

Kotter's Keys

John Kotter speaks of the new map as vision. For Kotter, vision is effective to clarify the direction of change. It "simplifies hundreds or thousands of more detailed decisions" and motivates teams to move in the right direction even if it's incredibly difficult: Teams that carry the same vision coordinate their efforts efficiently, without the need for constant communication.[14] A team that works from a common map doesn't have to check with the leader or a teammate before they make a move. Instead, individuals move with confidence and in the right direction.

Alignment is powerful for a team, enabling individual progress and preventing conflicting effort. Imagine two team members holding a two-by-four: If they face each other and move in opposite directions, they will waste energy by spinning in circles. Only when they agree on a destination are they able to move together.

Solving the problem of the old map is essential for building an effective disciplemaking team, but it takes time to embrace the new map. Don't expect to see it happen after one or two conversations. Remember, it took two hundred years for people to accept that California was not an island. How long has your church operated using the old map? The longer that map has been accepted as the truth, the harder it will be to change. If you accept something long enough, it becomes *the* way, not *a* way.

Clear vision requires three shared elements: a current location, a desired destination, and a plan for how to get there.

Drawing the New Map

In his book *The Advantage*, Patrick Lencioni offers six essential questions for developing clarity around a team's destination and road map. These six questions have proved effective in helping teams establish a new map. They are:

1. Why do we exist?
2. How do we behave?
3. What do we do?

4. How will we succeed?

5. What is most important, right now?

6. Who must do what?[15]

CORE teams that effectively work through these questions are able to establish common vision and purpose. The team leader isn't looking for people who already have a similar vision. Instead, the team will develop a common vision together. Then the CORE team will spread that vision to the rest of the church or ministry. A CORE team's answers to these questions might look something like this:

- *Why do we exist?* We exist to do, on a small scale, what we hope God will do on a larger scale in our ministry. We believe that a disciplemaking culture begins with a disciplemaking team—we are that team. To get there we need to reach two goals: First, we need to become a team. Second, we need to become disciplemakers who look, act, and speak like Jesus. As God molds and shapes us as individuals and as a team, we will be an example to others of what the lifestyle of a disciplemaker looks like.

- *How do we behave?* We behave like broken people who are becoming like Jesus, not just in our morals but also in our priorities, values, and methods. We humbly seek Him first. We are willing to be honest about our weaknesses without hiding behind them. We love one another enough to care and to confront, knowing that on both sides of confrontation we need to give and receive grace.

- *What do we do?* We love God first as we seek Him and remain obedient to His leading in our lives. We commit to loving one another and making disciples who make other disciples. We will make the team a priority and seek to be good teammates. We trust Him to birth a movement through us.

- *How will we succeed?* Our success comes from day-by-day surrender to Jesus and to one another. We cannot accomplish what God has called us to on our own. Our collective success is tied to our individual obedience. Our team's diversity—in age, gender, ethnicity, vocation, etc.—is important to our success. We are designed differently, and our diversity will allow us to impact different people. In that way, the fruitfulness of each individual can touch different networks within our church and community. Together our obedience proclaims that everyone is called to make disciples and that every disciple can reproduce as they journey to maturity.

The answers to the last two questions—*What is most important, right now?* and *Who must do what?*—change depending on the circumstances. At the beginning of the CORE team–building process, the most important priority is to get on the same page with regard to the common vision. This involves multiple conversations, rooted in Scripture, and encourages honest engagement from team members. As the team embraces the mission and begins to understand each other's gifts, the role each member is called to serve will be clarified. Members will begin to naturally rely on one another. The encouragers naturally pick up those who are struggling, the prophets naturally challenge the team to new levels of obedience, and the teachers explore ways to communicate and implement the best practices in disciplemaking.

It takes time to develop an effective CORE team. Creating clarity around these questions is the product of frequently praying together, wrestling with biblical truth, and having vulnerable conversations. Though it's easy to acknowledge the truth of what we should do, it's much more difficult to do the internal work necessary to become a living embodiment of that truth. In that work, God is with us.

No one likes to hear that his map shows an island that's really a peninsula. Any team that is not unified has no chance of healthy reproduction. However, a team with a common vision carries with it a pocket map that will guide the members as they encounter roadblocks, detours, and other unexpected challenges. When the destination is clear and the boundaries are defined, the trials shrink from insurmountable to manageable.

Spreading the New Map

Pastor Devin was working hard to build a disciplemaking culture in his church. He spent more time than usual on his four-week sermon series, "Be One, Make One." He wanted everyone to know that disciplemaking is relational and is for everyone. After the second week, he was encouraged. People seemed to be getting it! Each sermon was followed by a ten-minute testimony from a disciplemaker and the person she was discipling. Devin was sure it was working. That is, until he talked to Kayla.

Kayla, like the rest of the CORE team, had helped Devin plan the sermon series and was actively praying for its impact. She had only been a disciplemaker for six months, but she saw her life and her faith differently now. She called Pastor Devin because at her small group she had overheard a couple of women talking negatively about the previous Sunday's sermon. They said that disciplemaking was just the next church program and that they didn't want to do it. And they both wished Devin would stop pushing it.

Kayla reassured Devin that she hadn't heard disciplemaking come across as a program in his sermon, though others had. And then, before Devin could even ask her, she said, "Oh, I almost forgot. I made sure to tell them that this is relational and not just a passing program. Then I told them how it's helped me grow so much and that my time with Michelle is one of my favorite things in my life right now. They seemed genuinely interested, so I hope that helped them."

Devin thanked Kayla, then sat in his office processing what had just happened. At first, he was a bit frustrated that his sermons weren't getting through as much as he'd thought they would. But then he realized something amazing had just happened: Kayla was spreading the new map to others who were still following the old one! Devin realized that the CORE team was able to be in rooms and conversations that he could never be in himself. His excitement was so tangible that he said out loud, "Wow!"

Developing clarity around the map and the destination isn't enough. Clarity on the vision doesn't guarantee success. Success requires team members to own disciplemaking at a deep and personal level. Without that individual ownership, transformation doesn't happen. Individual ownership is what moves the CORE team from thinking to doing.

Reflection Questions

1. What is the main obstacle to developing a common vision?

2. What discipleship map has previously existed in your mind? In your church?

3. Write one or two paragraphs explaining the new disciplemaking map you'd like people to use.

4. What will you need to remember as you develop clarity around this vision?

5. Communicate what you've discovered to God. What next step is He asking you to take?

OWNED INDIVIDUALLY

Individual commitment to a group effort—that is what makes a team work, a company work, a society work, a civilization work.
VINCE LOMBARDI

Most disciplemaking leaders believe that if they develop clarity around the destination and the map, then people will go on the journey with them. No matter how much we wish that were the case, it's just not true.

It's counterintuitive, but our culture is full of examples of people who clearly see but don't move. Consider the sedentary person who knows all the risk factors associated with being out of shape yet still chooses to avoid regular exercise. Consider the person who sees the impact workaholism is having on their family yet continues to choose productivity over presence. Consider the pastor who knows he should observe the Sabbath but habitually answers nonemergency calls on his off day.

In fact, instead of moving someone to act, clarity has the potential to solidify a person's commitment to the status quo. How can this be? People simply do the math and decide the needed action isn't worth the effort. In disciplemaking, if nothing changes, then nothing changes.

Developing Individual Ownership

The connection between vision and action just can't be assumed. Why? Because people are intelligent, emotional, and committed to comfort. Consider the following examples of people who clearly see and believe in the mission yet still refuse to move.

1. Jonathan is a thirty-eight-year-old father of three who is living his life at capacity. He eagerly accepted the invitation to join the CORE team, and discussions at the team meetings convinced him that the current model of doing church isn't working. He listened to the arguments that the CORE team ought to be a disciplemaking foundation, but he remains unconvinced. Deep down Jonathan still believes that lasting change must ultimately come from church leadership.

   Jonathan is convinced about the problem but not the solution. As a result, he's not going to move. In meetings he affirms the direction, but he also looks for opportunities to propose staff-centric solutions.

2. Rachel is fifty-five, a new grandmother, and an established accountant. She has enjoyed the CORE team experience so far. But for decades, she has felt like something is off about

her church. It's clear to her now that a disciple can't just follow Jesus' moral teachings but must also follow His methods. What's become very clear to her during team meetings is the importance for a disciplemaker to be relational.

As a strong introvert Rachel is many things, but relational isn't one of them. She's convinced of the path forward, but she's equally convinced that her gifting and contribution are better directed elsewhere. Instead of relational disciplemaking, she wants to develop and lead events for young mothers and serve on the hospitality team. She's not really going to disciple anyone, but she is trying to intentionally invest in her family in order to fulfill her team responsibility.

3. Kevin is sixty-four, a longtime church elder, and one of the most respected people in the church. For decades he's led a small group and is currently leading an in-depth Sunday school class on the church fathers. Though a businessman by training, he invested years studying theology and the historical church. The CORE team conversations have challenged his convictions on how to make disciples. He's convinced that a relational approach would be very effective and more accessible to many people.

Yet Kevin isn't going to move either. He believes that God's equipped him to make disciples by using his gift of teaching in classes. He can think of many examples of individuals who have grown from his teaching. Not only that, he isn't interested in expending the extra time and energy necessary to try this relational approach. He's ready to support the team as they grow in this and to give modest effort, but he believes his best contribution is by doing what he's always done.

If you were leading a CORE team with these members, you might think that Jonathan, Rachel, and Kevin were fully on board. Each is faithful to the meetings and the assignments, and each encourages the general direction of disciplemaking. But none of them owns the vision individually. Each has a different reason for his or her passive resistance: Jonathan isn't convinced of the solution; Rachel doesn't think she's capable or called to develop that capability; and Kevin is unwilling to trade competence for incompetence. On the surface, they are on board, but in their hearts, they aren't open to moving toward relational disciplemaking. When leaders don't relationally track with the individuals on their team, they miss the truth of what's happening in the hearts of their team members.

How to Help Individuals Move

As you can see, clarity does not guarantee movement or ownership. One obstacle in a team setting is discerning between socially prompted action and action prompted by individual ownership. Only the latter carries a spark that will naturally spread to others.

Being a CORE team leader requires much more than simply leading team meetings and moving through content. The team leader must be willing to relationally invest in and love each team member. Love will pave the way for honest sharing. As George Washington Carver said, "Anything will give up its secrets if you love it enough."[1] Getting to that level of relational depth takes time, skill, and a good mix of challenge and encouragement. Challenge is key because encouragement alone is far more effective in helping actions continue rather than prompting new ones. Challenging a person helps him or her identify what needs to be changed. Leaders who love by both challenging and encouraging those they lead are able to develop vibrant relational connections that yield amazing fruit.

Cultivating connections strong enough to develop individual ownership requires the leader to move toward team members even when everything is going well. Since many leaders lead at or over capacity, this aspect of CORE team leadership is often neglected. Be warned: Such neglect threatens the entire process. Since teams are only as strong as their weakest link, a team with one person who isn't fully on board changes the culture of the entire team.

Pastor Drew learned this lesson the hard way. He started his CORE team with eight eager members. After over a year of hard work and investment, only half had embraced relational disciplemaking. The other four had stayed on the team and supported the general movement of disciplemaking, but they did not practice it themselves. As Drew and I evaluated what had happened, it became clear that he hadn't cultivated relationships with the team to really know why those team members weren't discipling others.

Afterward, Drew decided to try again. He formed a new CORE team and was determined to check in with each team member at least once a month. His goal was to have at least one monthly ten-minute conversation with each member. If he sensed someone was struggling, he would meet with that person for a longer period of time. He started off strong, but similar results to those in the past eventually led him to discover that he'd been neglecting those check-ins for months. There were reasons, of course—staff issues, family challenges, and the usual swirl of ministry. Drew was discouraged, but he wasn't disheartened.

On his third attempt, Drew kept his focus on the individual members of the CORE team, checking in regularly and challenging and encouraging them as needed. This time, it worked. This CORE team embraced the vision of disciplemaking not just in principle but in practice.

Individual ownership is critical to the success of a team. Team leaders must do the relational work in order to help individuals get through the barriers they face during the process. In order for a team leader to do this successfully, he needs to make it a high priority, build sufficient time in his schedule, and protect that time from intrusion.

Most of all, the leader must *actually* love the team members. Forced care is worse than no care at all. Super Bowl–winning coach Jimmy Johnson stated it this way: "The only thing worse than a coach or CEO who doesn't care about his people is one who pretends to care. People can spot a phony every time. They know he doesn't care about them, and worse, his act insults their intelligence."[2] A team leader who truly cares for the individuals on the team will build strong relationships that can support the weight of dissent, disagreement, and dissatisfaction.

A Coach Approach to Ownership

When team members struggle to own the vision, team leaders can use coaching conversations to draw them out and move them forward. Sometimes known as *motivational interviewing,* this tool helps individuals identify their current reality, desired future, barriers, and next steps.

It helps to visualize these conversations as a bridge from your current reality to a desired future. The bridge itself is made by conquering barriers through concrete action steps. (A more complete explanation of this coaching framework can be found in appendix B.) The concrete action steps prompt movement from thought to action and grow internal motivation.[3] It's difficult to overstate the power that imagining the destination, naming the obstacles, and planning how to overcome them has for those who struggle to get going. Leaders who use coaching conversations and link accountability to action steps often see team members transform rapidly.

Leaders must also recognize that individual objections are just that—individual. While addressing individual obstacles in the context of the team is sometimes appropriate, most of the time it's better for the leader to address them with just one or two people. Addressing these matters in small relational contexts away from the team has several advantages.

First, this allows a team member to deal with his own obstacles without worrying about what others may think. Whether the obstacles stem from a weakness or a difference of opinion, individual conversations with the team leader allow each person to be heard in a relational context. No one wants to be singled out for not getting something.

Second, addressing these matters in a relational way allows the leader to model a disciplemaking context for the team member. As the leader listens and patiently instructs, the team member experiences the power of disciplemaking in real time. Such an experience helps team members who have never been discipled to "get it" much faster.

Third, when individual obstacles are addressed outside a team meeting, it clearly and continually proclaims the team's purpose by keeping the focus on topics that bring about a common connection and shared growth.

Individual ownership is important because the conviction to make disciples must be bigger than the individual. In other words, each person's fear must be smaller than the conviction to multiply. As Jesus says in John 12:24, "Very truly I tell you, unless a kernel of wheat falls to the ground and dies, it remains only a single seed. But if it dies, it produces many seeds." When team members are willing to step through their fears, they can step into the fruitfulness of reproduction. The CORE team is designed to support each person as they overcome their obstacles by putting them in relationship with others who are also being stretched and transformed. The momentum of that transformation drives the team toward a new lifestyle and the acquisition of new competencies.

Jesus' Example

Jesus was (and still is) a master at developing individual ownership. From the start Jesus called individuals to follow Him and to pursue the mission He saw and defined for them.[4]

What's not as clear in the Scriptures is the real-world response to Jesus' call. For instance, it appears in Matthew 4:20 that Peter dropped everything and followed the first time he met Jesus. But as we see in John 1–4, Peter frequently traveled with Jesus far from his Capernaum home for about a year before the call in Matthew 4:20. These trips in and out of town with Jesus would have put some stress on Peter and his family. It's fair to assume that while he was gone, he wasn't able to financially provide for his family in the same way as when he was there to fish. Was there financial stress in Peter's life and family as a result of his travels with Jesus? Did he feel pulled in many directions during the first year of relating to Jesus? We don't know for sure, but you don't have to squint to see the signs of such things.

Consider Luke 5. Peter has been out fishing all night and hasn't caught anything. But not catching anything is an insufficient description of what happened to Peter that night. Peter spent hour after hour after hour after hour throwing his nets into the water and pulling them out with nothing in them. He was on his home lake, the Sea of Galilee, so he must have gone to favorite spot after favorite spot after favorite spot. And he didn't catch anything! That's frustrating enough, but imagine having that experience when you *needed* to catch some fish. Imagine having that experience when you had limited time to fish because you'd been traveling with Jesus and money was low and there were bills coming due. Not only would that night have been physically draining, but it would have been even more emotionally draining.

In the morning, Peter sits in his boat cleaning his nets when he hears Jesus down the beach teaching a crowd. I wonder what Peter felt when he noticed Jesus. I wonder what Jesus was teaching about that morning. Maybe He was teaching about how God cares for and provides for His children—one of Jesus' favorite topics. Would you blame Peter if he felt some frustration hearing Jesus teach about that after such an exhausting night? Peter may have been trying to clean those nets in record time so he could get out of there and go home to sleep!

But then, as the crowd pushes in close to Jesus, He asks Peter to use his boat. Jesus jumps in and pushes out a bit from the shore to continue His teaching. After what seems like an eternity, Jesus wraps up His teaching. Instead of getting out of the boat, Jesus looks at Peter and says something like "Hey, Peter, why don't we go out for a catch? It's such a nice morning!"

There's no sign of grumbling from Peter. He takes the boat out with his freshly cleaned nets. Peter is tired and knows there's no fish to be caught, but he goes. Finally, they get to the deep, and Peter throws his net into the water. When he starts to pull it out, he is shocked to find that there's something in it. As he pulls harder, he realizes the net is very heavy. He may have looked at Jesus in that moment of shock. I like to imagine Jesus with a big, knowing smile on His face. And as Peter pulls with all his might, he realizes he needs help. He calls out to his friends. Together they get the fish into the boat. So. Many. Fish. The boat begins to sink in the water from their sheer weight. And then . . . something strange happens. Instead of reacting with excitement, Peter falls at Jesus' feet. Instead of going to Jesus with joy, instead of saying thanks a hundred times, Peter tells the Lord to go away because he is a sinful man. But why?

Let me be clear: We don't know for sure. But I think we need to work with what we do know to shed light on what we don't. We know that Peter had been traveling with Jesus for about a year. We know that when one family member is gone, it puts pressure on the rest of the family. We know that something had motivated

Peter to be out fishing all night long. We know that flopping all around Peter in that moment was something like a year's worth of wages if the fish were sold at market. And Peter responded with what appears to be remorse or shame or guilt.

I believe that Peter had been struggling to trust Jesus to provide for his and his family's needs. I believe that he was struggling to fully surrender to Jesus, that his transformation from ordinary faith to walk-on-water faith took some time to develop. If you ask me, the fishing trip was more about catching Peter for the mission than it was about catching fish.

This is an incredible example of Jesus caring enough about Peter to help him trust God and own the mission. A few other examples of Jesus' care for the disciples include asking them to feed the five thousand, sending them out two by two to preach and drive out demons, and challenging their independence when they couldn't drive out a demon.

Jesus' way of making disciples makes it clear that change is often the fruit of challenge. He combined everyday encouragement and connection with regular confrontation. Jesus was able to confront because He was close enough to know where to aim the challenge. That closeness was the fruit of trust. The disciples knew He cared more about them as individuals than about any agenda He had for them. Team leaders who wish to develop ownership must be close enough to their people to do the same.

Kotter's Keys

John Kotter (first mentioned in chapter 3) approaches ownership by talking about driving out complacency, developing a willingness to sacrifice for the desired change, and making clear the impact of doing nothing. These are ingredients of individual ownership. In *Leading Change*, he says, "Major change is usually impossible unless most employees are willing to help, often to the point of making short-term sacrifices. But people will not make sacrifices, even if they are unhappy with the status quo, unless they think the potential benefits of change are attractive and unless they really believe that a transformation is possible. Without credible communication, and a lot of it, employees' hearts and minds are never captured."[5]

Kotter argues that complacency is the enemy of new cultural initiatives because complacency kills urgency. Urgency leads to sacrificial human effort (which is a helpful characterization of ownership). Kotter's approach to creating urgency is to challenge the status quo and the future that will result from it. He calls on people to buy into a different vision that will create a different future. When they buy into that different vision, they are poised to make specific changes and sacrifices. Kotter's approach bears some similarity to Jesus'. When urgency is high, people are motivated to give extra effort and take needed steps to make their vision a reality.[6]

Developing this level of ownership is individual work that runs counter to leadership muscle memory. That muscle memory is the result of training and experience. It says that change starts by rewriting vision and mission statements, setting new goals, and supporting that work with carrot-and-stick incentives. But working on organizational levers first, before individuals, is backward execution. Culture change specialist J. Stewart Black has learned that "lasting success comes from changing individuals first and then using organizational levers to sustain the change."[7] Organizational levers have power to change people at the level of behavior, but they rarely impact beliefs. Beliefs are changed on an individual level through targeted challenges, conversations, and experiences. When you do the work of developing a CORE team, your efforts result in individual ownership. Team members are then unleashed within the culture, which can change as the organization adjusts.

Changing without Changing Anything

Team members who own the vision are a progress marker on the road to culture change. There are many ways the team leader can observe such ownership. The story I told in chapter 5 about Kayla intervening on her pastor's behalf is one example. Let me share another with you.

Jack had been on the CORE team for about nine months. His attendance wasn't the best because of a demanding job in health care, but he made it when he could and was always very engaged when he was there. He was the sort of guy who brought intensity wherever he went. For six months, he had trouble seeing what this disciplemaking thing was all about. It seemed like what he'd been doing all along: loving God, serving others, and so on. Each time the team meetings rolled around, he wondered if it was even worth going. Still, he showed up and tried to understand.

Matt, the team leader, faithfully sought regular time with Jack. At least once a month before the service, he called or talked to Jack about the team and how he was doing. It took a while before Jack admitted he really didn't get what all the fuss was about. Wasn't this the stuff they'd been doing all along? Matt listened, then asked Jack if he'd ever asked the people he served with on the welcoming team how their time in the Word was going. Jack hadn't. Matt didn't press further but instead let the question sit with Jack.

In the coming days, Jack couldn't stop thinking about that question. So the next week, he asked a couple of the guys about their time in the Word. He was amazed to find that they hadn't really been reading the Bible that week. Jack encouraged them to get into it and promised he'd ask them the next week. As he asked them and encouraged them, they started reading the Bible regularly. Jack was so excited that he told Matt.

Matt was so encouraged, and then he asked Jack, "Okay, so what now with them?"

Little by little, Jack started to take on the role of spiritual father to these guys. He invited them into a disciplemaking relationship. He also began to lead the others on the welcoming team differently. Jack had changed, but in another way, he hadn't really changed anything. He wasn't serving somewhere new. He hadn't changed the number of hours he volunteered. And he didn't change how they welcomed people on Sunday morning.

On the other hand, everything had changed. Jack changed how he interacted with each person on the welcome team. He asked different questions. He shared different stories. And he had his antenna up for how he could encourage and ask questions that would help people move toward God.

Finally, Jack went up to Matt and said, "I get it now. Disciplemaking makes everything different. I've been circling it all along, but now I'm focused and intentional about it."

The Ownership Journey Leads to Conviction

When disciplemakers own the mission deeply, something amazing happens: People who have sat passively on the sidelines for years start to get very hungry to multiply. They are no longer content to leave the real work of disciplemaking to the professionals and spiritual superstars. Instead, they own their relationship with God and His mission for them and soon become powerful disciplemakers.

They also carry within them strong convictions about what the fulfilled vision will look like and how the team can get there. For some, those convictions will come out proactively—in the form of opinions and directives. For others, they will come out reactively in the form of pushback against the opinions and directives of others. This mix of convictions, actions, and reactions leads to friction on a team. And if the tension isn't handled well, teams can crumble. In the next chapter, we'll take a look at how teams become relationally resilient.

Reflection Questions

1. When have you been convinced of a better way but remained committed to your status quo? Why?

2. When did you know you "owned" Jesus-style disciplemaking for yourself?

3. What types of passive resistance to disciplemaking have you seen in your church? How could you address each of these types?

4. What will you need to remember as you help each CORE team member own the vision?

5. Communicate what you've discovered to God. What next step is He asking you to take?

RELATIONALLY RESILIENT

"Love one another. As I have loved you, so you must love one another. By this everyone will know that you are my disciples, if you love one another."

JESUS, JOHN 13:34-35

In 2006, designer Peter Skillman presented the results of a competition called the Marshmallow Challenge (which has since been repeated thousands of times around the world as a team-building exercise). Skillman evaluated the success of groups of CEOs, lawyers, business school students, and even kindergartners. In this activity, each four-person team has eighteen minutes to build the tallest freestanding structure possible using the following materials:

- twenty pieces of uncooked spaghetti
- one yard of string
- one yard of transparent tape
- one regular-size marshmallow

Apart from the time constraint, the only rule is that "the marshmallow must end up on top."[1]

As you might expect, there was a big difference between the results of the adults and those of the kindergartners. For the four groups mentioned above, the average heights in inches were as follows: 10, 16, 21, and 26.[2] Care to guess the order? From worst to first, the results were business school students, lawyers, CEOs, and kindergartners.[3]

Yes, the kids were the big winners of this challenge! How did the kids consistently outperform so many highly educated adults? How can groups of six-year-olds build towers that average over twice the height of those built by business school students? The answer offers us a key to developing relationally resilient teams.

The surprising results spurred further study. Out of the many differences in team makeup, which ones are most important to the outcome? Clearly, adults possess a much stronger grasp of strategy, physics, and respect for others. Despite this, researchers concluded that what makes kids' teams so successful is how they collaborate.

Each adult team starts in essentially the same way. They talk about the problem, formulate a strategy, throw out design ideas, divide up tasks—maybe even appoint a CEO of Spaghetti, Inc.!

Kids don't do any of that. Instead of talking about the problem or asking for each other's ideas, they simply grab materials and get to work. As they go along, they take materials from each other and communicate abruptly: "Give me that." "No, you can't." "Wait! Just let me!" An observer might describe their winning strategy as quickly finding a bad solution, then finding a slightly better one—and repeating as needed.

It's not that kids' teams collaborate and others don't, but rather their style of collaboration reveals each team's top priorities:

- The adults' top priority tends to be managing the status and emotions of each person in the group.
- The kids' top priority tends to be building the tallest tower possible.

While kindergartners get right to work building their tower, adults busy themselves trying to understand: "*Who is in charge? Is it okay to criticize someone else's idea? What are the rules here?*"[4] Or *How do I contribute without upsetting my teammates?*

The essential difference between the older participants and the kids was not their individual skills but the way they interacted. This is an important lesson because on a CORE team, the relational culture carries within it a base code for its true priorities and values.

The Challenge of Developing a Relationally Resilient Team

Relationships are hard. If that's not self-evident, consider the fact that 41 percent of first-time marriages end in divorce.[5] That means that four out of ten people who take time to look all over and find that one person they're crazy about—and who's crazy about them—end up discovering that this person is someone with whom they can't maintain a relationship!

CORE team relationships are obviously very different from marriage, but to be successful both require commitment. As team members buy into the vision and start to own it, team relationships become more complicated. The team whose participants started at roughly the same disciplemaking place now has individuals at various places with regard to seeing, owning, and acting on the vision. Those who haven't struggled can become frustrated with those who lag behind, while those who are struggling can react negatively when they feel like they aren't getting it. This is on top of the intentional gender, generational, and ethnic differences that were built in from the start. The CORE team becomes a petri dish in which conflict and relational tension easily grow.

The presence of relational issues is actually a good sign. It's counterintuitive, but with all the differences on the team, relational challenges are an indicator that team members are engaging with one another as teammates, not just as group members. Still, if the team leader doesn't intentionally shepherd the team members through relational tension, that tension can grow into a problem that sabotages the entire culture-building process.

For this reason, team leaders have to be aware of relational tension between team members. Relationally resilient teams are the result of Christlike relationships and Christlike leadership. Jesus taught that the disciples' relationships with one another would prove to outsiders their love for Him.[6] The same is true for the CORE team as they relate to the broader ministry and to the outside world.

The team must be committed to loving each other like Jesus. They must be more devoted to individual development than to team harmony and also more devoted to building a Christlike people than to having a peaceful culture.

It's easier said than done. Healthy relationships require honest communication in order to foster honest connection. Teams whose members relate to one another in polite, stilted ways (like colleagues or group members) miss the conflict and tension that loving and being loved produces. If the CORE team can't really love one another, how can they hope to love others? Relational resilience is the by-product of loving one another into and through the misunderstandings and hurt that relationships can produce.

The team leader is the determining factor in whether team members will connect enough to produce tension or instead remain at a polite distance from one another. She will set the pace by how she relates to the team inside and outside team meetings. When someone says something insensitive, will it be addressed? When someone misses meetings without communicating to the team, how will that be handled? When a team member struggles with a family crisis, how will the team leader respond and lead the teammates to respond?

When the leader notices relational tension developing between team members, she must proactively help them work through it. This is a great challenge for leaders who prefer to run from or ignore conflict—a response that's typical in our culture. But when *becoming just like Jesus* is the goal, then loving people like Jesus is essential.

Cultivating the team's culture is essential if the CORE team is going to have something valuable to offer the larger church/ministry culture. Longtime NBA coach Gregg Popovich knows a few things about building a healthy team culture. Between 1980 and 2014, Popovich was the NBA's best coach as measured by wins over expectation, holding the title by a wide margin over such legendary coaches as George Karl (33 fewer games won over expectation) and the oft-celebrated Phil Jackson (62 fewer games over expectation).[7] Popovich's longtime assistant coach Chip Engelland described his style this way: "A lot of coaches can yell or be nice, but what Pop does is different. He delivers two things over and over: He'll tell you the truth . . . and then he'll love you to death."[8]

Popovich did what Jesus demonstrated by maintaining a high standard while at the same time loving his team when they failed to meet that standard. Grace and truth probably aren't new concepts for you, but combining them in the way you engage your CORE team members may be.

If leaders want a CORE team with a culture worth exporting, they must be willing to maintain the team's standards as they praise the positive and point out the negative. This is done in the context of genuine relationships. Leaders are often pushed out of their comfort zone in giving both positive and corrective feedback. Many pastors struggle with people pleasing; it's natural for anyone to shy away from giving a needed admonition to a volunteer, especially if that volunteer is in charge of their job review! Despite the challenge, Christian leaders are called to speak the truth plainly as those who ultimately answer to God. They are also called to follow that truth telling with love and concern communicated by leaning into relationship. Such an example communicates expectations to the team and establishes trust in the leader.

When clear feedback is paired with grace, people feel safe to be who they are as they move toward becoming what they're meant to be. Leaders can repeatedly communicate grace-filled messages to the team by sharing their own personal struggles, weaknesses, and failures while inviting the team's help. That help can take many familiar forms, such as accountability and encouragement as well as instruction from others who are strong in those areas. Alternatively, leaders who are unable to give clear feedback—positive and negative—tend to produce teams that are pulled down by one or two individuals (such as a complainer, an over-talker, or an aggressive truth teller). Leaders must be intentional in addressing situations like these, because if they're left unaddressed, they will slowly erode the team's trust in the leader and the process.

Keys to Helpful Feedback

Two keys to achieving clear and helpful feedback are (1) *relationship capital* and (2) *focusing the feedback* in the context of team performance.

As we saw in the last chapter, investing in team members is essential. The team leader needs to build relational capital in order for the team to hear critique without becoming defensive. But let me emphasize: Developing a relational connection with the primary motivation of building relational capital is manipulation and will normally backfire! At least once a month, the team leader needs to find margin and emotional bandwidth to intentionally connect and converse with each team member. The connection should be face-to-face or in pairs with respect to the opposite gender. As relationships grow, a leader's genuine care and compassion for each team member grows also. The team leader's capacity to build these personal relationships should limit the size of the CORE team.

The second key is to focus feedback in the context of the team's performance. Feedback conversations give team members the opportunity to voice personal struggles such as insecurity, lack of follow-through, and obstacles they must overcome to go where they feel God is leading them. For team leaders, feedback conversations provide the opportunity to give input to each individual. One common issue that a leader should speak into is a team member's insecurity that is impacting the team. This manifests in that person either refusing to speak up or speaking up so much he or she becomes a "know-it-all." While the former robs the team of vital contribution and unity, the latter robs the team of robust discussion and individual value.

Direct feedback helps each person understand the impact he is having on the team and gives him a chance to adjust. In each case, the leader is responsible to address the myriad issues threatening the team's progress. These crucial conversations can help team members grow. The sad reality is that most adults have never had someone who cared enough to lovingly speak the truth about how they are impacting others. The desire to love like Jesus motivates the team leader to have these very difficult and very personal conversations.

Unfortunately, fear and a lack of love can lead team leaders to avoid these conversations. It's not okay for a disciplemaking leader to allow team members to negatively impact other team members to the point where those same team members talk poorly about and avoid them because of these experiences. The examples are abundant, and you can probably picture people you have known who came off as know-it-alls, complainers, or passive-aggressive, or who exhibited other connection-destroying behaviors. Team leaders must be loving enough and courageous enough to address these behaviors. When they do, they open up doors to connection and transformation that speak volumes about the desired culture.

Handling Conflict

Though conflict is a normal part of healthy relationships, many avoid it at all costs. Avoiding conflict in order to keep the peace makes the problem bigger and will typically result in the loss of one or more team members who are involved in the conflict. However, when conflict is handled well, trust and relational depth grow. Conflict really can be an opportunity for growth and greater connection.

Jesus was committed to peacemaking, not to peacekeeping.[9] The difference is huge. As my friend Lou says, "Conflict is always about leadership because leadership is always about character." Leaders must learn to handle conflict head-on. Remember, the CORE team is a microcosm of your desired church culture. If you are the team leader, you can model biblical peacemaking. If team members aren't handling conflict biblically, boldly step in to ensure that the conflict doesn't splash onto the entire team. Appropriately handling conflict is a life skill essential to a reproducing disciple. Developing that life skill in your team members will help them in their families, their workplaces, and their friendships.

A healthy team culture will bring to the surface sin and immaturity in the same way that a marriage does. Teams seeking to bury these things will not develop the disciplemaking culture they seek. Instead, they will develop a culture that values comfort over character. Team members will relate to one another, themselves, and the world in a fractured way that aims at self-protection. An unsuccessful CORE team engages one another, the church, and the world on the basis of what's best for each individual. The CORE team must learn to behave as anti-consumers—as those who seek to serve instead of being served, who seek to solve problems rather than simply identifying them, and who seek to help others grow, not just themselves. They must become surrendered disciples.

Jesus' Example

Examples of conflict among the disciples are few, but Mark 9:33-40 tells us how Jesus handled two contentious situations on His team.[10]

Here's my paraphrase of what happened. After walking to Capernaum with his disciples, Jesus initiated a conversation with them that went something like this:

"Hey, guys, what were you arguing about back there?"

(Silence, likely because they felt too ashamed to admit they'd been arguing about who would be greatest in the Kingdom of Heaven.)

"All right, gather around. We need to have a talk. Guys, if anyone wants to be first or great, then he must become everyone's servant."

"Okay, Jesus, so who is the greatest in the Kingdom of Heaven, then?"

"Look at this child here. Unless you welcome her, then you'll never even get into heaven. But whoever humbles himself and welcomes a child will be the greatest in the Kingdom of Heaven."

What can we learn about Jesus' leadership from this conversation? First, when Jesus became aware of conflict on His team, He didn't avoid it. He initiated a conversation about the argument.

Second, He helped the disciples refocus on Kingdom values and priorities.

CORE team leaders need to do the same. When (not if) conflict arises on the team, the team leader needs to actively engage those involved, help them sort it out, and then help them focus on the common vision that they are pursuing together as teammates.

In the second situation in Mark 9 (starting in verse 38), the disciples tell Jesus about a man who used Jesus' name to drive out demons. The disciples tried to stop him because he wasn't part of their group. Jesus responds by correcting their thinking, telling them that no one can do a miracle in His name and then turn around and speak bad of Him. He also adds that anyone who isn't against them is for them.

The same lesson applies to CORE teams, since they often bump into a similar situation. They find someone in the church or ministry who is talking about or doing disciplemaking but isn't connected to the team. So instead of being concerned (like the disciples were) about what others are doing in the name of Jesus, CORE team members may become concerned about what others are doing in the name of "discipleship." If team members handle their concerns like the disciples handled theirs, they might discourage a fellow disciple from discipling others because he or she doesn't know enough or doesn't know the "right" way to do it. Team leaders must be alert to this because a whole culture of disciplemaking is big enough to accommodate different methods of discipling as long as they are upheld by the same principles.

Kotter's Keys

Kotter addresses team relationships, but in the context of the business world. In that environment, individuals are invested in the change process because they want to keep their jobs and perhaps advance to higher positions. Those who are unwilling to respond to the team leader's directives are typically replaced by someone who will. The person being replaced usually leaves the organization entirely and no longer impacts the work. In ministry, relationships are primary, not secondary. Members are volunteers and clients at the same time. As a result, difficult people must be developed, not disposed of, and the development must be done in a way that deepens the relational and missional connection.

Even with these differences, Kotter recognizes the need for trust among team members. He says, "Only teams with the right composition and sufficient trust among members can be highly effective."[11] As with the ad hoc tower-building teams at the beginning of the chapter, there's no getting around the fact that teams that communicate honestly and maintain solid relationships get more done faster.

If your team has difficulty working together, then Kotter suggests it may be due to a lack of trust on the team. He says, "When trust is present, you will usually be able to create teamwork. When it is missing you won't."[12] This sounds simple, but when you are in the midst of frustrating meetings where the team seems to be "missing something," this is a valuable insight.

Lastly, Kotter notes the impact that "small" relational problems can have on the overall objective, especially when other problems emerge. He observes, "Personnel problems that can be ignored during easy times can cause serious trouble in a tougher, faster-moving, globalizing economy."[13]

Charlie's Dilemma

Mason had been leading his CORE team for two months. So far everything was just okay. He wasn't totally sure the meetings were hitting the mark. He typically felt that the ninety minutes flew by. He wanted his team members to connect personally, but he also wanted them to have time to really dig into the material.

At the last meeting, he'd decided to refocus everyone on the team's goals: (1) to become a team, and (2) to become disciple-makers. As he talked, he mentioned how important it was for each person to be committed to preparation and to the team meetings. He reminded everyone to put the dates in their calendar for the next year. "Let's make sure we are here, even if we have to move stuff to make this a priority," he said.

The next week Mason received an email from Charlie. Charlie was a deeply faithful and diligent man in his early sixties. He told Mason that he needed to step off the team because he had several conflicts in the coming months that he couldn't move. Charlie and his wife were going to see their daughter and newly born grandchild two states over in the coming month. Two weeks after that, he would have a knee-replacement procedure. A month after that, his nephew was getting married, and he would be out of town again. Charlie's list of conflicts stretched eight months out. He wasn't going to miss every meeting, but he'd miss six out of eight.

Mason was ready to let him off the hook, but as they talked, he sensed that Charlie still wanted to be on the team. Given the nature of his conflicts and Charlie's desire, Mason suggested that they talk it over as a team at the next meeting.

Mason opened the next meeting with Charlie's situation. He set up the conversation, then gave Charlie the floor to explain that he had a deep desire to be on the team but felt he wouldn't be a good teammate because of his other commitments.

Mason asked the team, "How do you think we should handle this?"

Greg was the first to respond. "Sounds like all those conflicts are reasons, not excuses. I think he should be allowed to continue." A few others echoed the sentiment.

Mason added, "I agree, but it's going to be hard for Charlie to feel like he's part of the team when he's missing so often. And what about him continuing to develop into a disciplemaker?"

This time, Brian spoke first. "Well, I would be willing to catch him up on what he misses each time. We could meet in person or some other way."

Carrie picked it up from there. "And we see each other at church a lot. As a team we could be intentional about checking in with him there. It sounds like he'll have a lot of opportunities to engage others, right?"

Mason had hoped something like this would happen. He thanked them for their input and looked to Charlie. "Well, what do you think?"

Charlie said, "I think this is a team I don't want to leave."

Conclusion

The stretching that healthy relationships cause is important to our maturation process. CORE teams that relate to one another with grace and honesty love each other *through* conflict. Relational resilience is difficult but doable. As the team continues to move toward the end of the CORE team–building process, an interesting thing happens: The leader and the members start to perceive reality very differently from how they did before. The divergence brings into view the next big obstacle on the team's journey: finishing.

Reflection Questions

1. What allowed kids to outperform adults in the building competition described in this chapter?

2. How do you normally respond to conflict or potential conflict? What does this reveal about your view of conflict?

3. Write a paragraph explaining the difference between peacemaking and peacekeeping.

4. What will you need to remember as you help the CORE team become relationally resilient?

5. Communicate what you've discovered to God. What next step is He asking you to take?

ENDURE TO THE END

I didn't come this far to only come this far.
UNKNOWN

In the end, sculptor Bonanno Pisano left his tower leaning and incomplete (see chapters 1 and 4). Despite years of effort and the expectation of success, once he faced an obstacle that seemed insurmountable, Pisano did what people often do: He walked away, having buried the stone that proclaimed his brilliance. In his mind, the failure left him no choice.

It's easy to empathize with Pisano. We all know what it's like to try our best, fail, and then quit. Every year millions make resolutions that follow the same narrative. We begin, persuaded that we need to change. We're convinced that we can do what's needed to make the change. Then we start living into that change. Finally, we tire of the new way, and we quit. Quitting is as human as trying.

A Different Experience

At this point in the process, some CORE team members are ready to quit.

CORE team members have been challenged together, frustrated together, and changed together. Individuals have seen the distortions of the old map and have bought into the new map. They traded competence and confidence in the old way for incompetence and reticence in the face of a steep learning curve. They were convinced that to create change, they needed to be changed. They worked with other teammates toward individual and collective disciplemaking fruitfulness.

As they pressed on, they were still trying to make it all work. But now they feel worn out. In this phase many teams feel like they have been on a days-long car ride. The desire to just "be out of the car" grows stronger by the day. At times, it feels like the final destination is still a million miles away. The journey to competence is hard for anyone, especially for the high-functioning adults typically invited onto a CORE team. They are used to having it all together and excelling. It's been a long time since they were beginners, and they don't like it.

The combination of low proficiency and poor results is a dangerous one. Many feel a strong desire to quit. It's not that they necessarily think they should be doing better; it's more that they don't trust their own ability. Each team has some members who struggle with doubts. They often sound like this: *Perhaps I'm not able to do this after all. Maybe my leader was wrong about this being the right way to go. My teammates look like they are better at this than I am. Maybe I'm just not suited for this. I feel like I'm holding the team back. They would be better off if I just stepped aside.* Believing someone else can make disciples is one thing; believing *you* can is something else entirely!

Team members at risk of quitting aren't hard to identify. They start to disengage by missing meetings or by not participating in meetings they attend. The vision that they had so clearly seen is now leaky. When they talk about disciplemaking, they lack conviction and passion. And most of all, they doubt their own ability to make a disciple and God's desire to do it through them.

If you observe these signs in a team member, he needs you *now*. He needs you to enter into his struggle and to remind him of what God has done and is doing in him. But don't wait—if you do, he might quit before you talk to him!

What makes this phase so difficult to navigate is that while team members struggle silently, the team leader is energized by progress, momentum, and a glimpse of the destination. Being in a state of excitement makes it easy for the team leader to miss the signs of exhaustion in the team members. After all, he's led them through this process. So even if team leaders are fatigued too, they're probably more enthusiastic than tired. Most have ministered for decades and never had everyday disciples like these who are deeply committed to the same vision of making disciples where they live, work, and worship. The combination of the leader's excitement and the team's exhaustion makes this a crucial time for everyone.

What's clear is this: If the team's vulnerability isn't recognized, the unaware team leader will turn his attention away from personally ministering to the team members and toward organizational levers (such as a discipleship pathway, funding the mission, etc.).

This is a mistake. Moving away from the relational check-ins will result in a team that disintegrates from the inside out.

The leader must lead the team through this valley. The reason is simple: Even though there's a lot to be encouraged by (to continue with the car trip metaphor), the team is still days away from the final destination—nothing less than a disciplemaking culture that will impact the greater (non-Christian) culture.

To lead effectively through this phase, a leader needs to aggressively encourage each team member by doing two things: (1) celebrating how far the team member has come and (2) reminding the team member of the bigger vision they've been called to fulfill. As the leader draws attention toward these milestones and goals, he also needs to *increase* the amount of time and attention he gives to the team members. Doing these things will make the conquered obstacles and the distance left to travel look smaller.

Jesus' Example

The endurance that Jesus' team of disciples needed is obvious. In the nine months prior to the cross, Jesus intentionally prepared His team of disciples for the suffering that was coming. Not only would they spend their final months with Jesus in an increasingly hostile environment, but they would also experience events that defied expectations.

The new map they had to grasp was nearly incomprehensible to them. Instead of cultivating a following, Jesus would appear to send people away.[1] Instead of prevailing and ruling over His earthly enemies, He would be beaten and killed by them. Instead of turning evil on its head, He would appear to be overtaken by it. The disciples not only had to witness these events, but they also had to deal with the impact of them. It's easy to hear their thoughts from two thousand years away: *Maybe He isn't who we thought He was. If He really was the promised Messiah, it wouldn't be this way.* The temptation to turn away from Him and from the calling was so strong that some doubted even after His resurrection.[2]

Jesus knew that for His team of disciples to survive, they would need to have unbreakable faith in Him and in the greater call on their lives. In teaching His disciples to endure, He modeled for us how to equip a team of disciples to endure hardship and doubt.

The first and most important thing He did to prepare them was to draw them close relationally. In fact, as the end of His human life drew near, His time with them increased. His proximity to the Twelve affirmed His invitation to them years earlier to "be with him."[3] He also helped them see the progress they had made together. He did this by explicitly telling them how their relationship had grown over the years: from servants to friends.[4] Their relationship with Jesus was the model from which they were to understand what it meant to love one another and others.[5]

The relational connection was also strengthened in a context of rest. Jesus intentionally found ways for the team to rest together. The shared rest allowed their relationships to deepen as they nurtured each other. He took them away from the everyday pressures and demands of ministry to remote places. They took retreats in every region they traveled: Tyre and Sidon (Matthew 15:21; Mark 7:24); the Decapolis border (Matthew 15:29; Mark 7:31); Dalmanutha in southwest Galilee (Mark 8:10); the villages of Caesarea Philippi (Matthew 16:13; Mark 8:27); Perea, east of the

Jordan (John 10:40–11:54; Luke 13:22; 19:28); and Ephraim near the desert because the hostility was too great in Judea (John 11:54).[6]

Second, Jesus repeatedly put the big picture in front of the disciples—the same thing He did to encourage Himself as He headed to the cross.[7] In those final nine months, Jesus spoke at least ten times about returning to His heavenly home.[8] As the coming storm approached, Jesus wanted His team to know they could still trust Him. Though the disciples didn't fully grasp these things, the Gospels show how important these reminders were to their faith after the Resurrection.

Third, Jesus wanted them to see who they had become and who they would become. He prayed within their hearing about how they were sent to Him by the Father, that they had obeyed the word, that they were not of the world any more than He was, that they were being sent into the world, and that many would believe through their message.[9] He told them of the coming Holy Spirit, who would not only remind them of Jesus' teachings but also provide guidance and peace. He told them that they would do even greater things than He had done, that they could move mountains, and that they would have complete joy.[10]

Fourth, Jesus challenged them to carry on. Just three months before the cross, in one of His most pointed teachings on endurance (and very relevant to this book), He said in Luke 14:28-30, "Suppose one of you wants to build a tower. Won't you first sit down and estimate the cost to see if you have enough money to complete it? For if you lay the foundation and are not able to finish it, everyone who sees it will ridicule you, saying, 'This person began to build and wasn't able to finish.'"

His message to the disciples was clear: *I love you. I have prepared you for the road ahead. You have what it takes, so keep going.* Team leaders need to help each team member absorb the same message: *I love you. You are prepared for this. You have what it takes. Keep going.*

Kotter's Keys

Again, as a businessman, Kotter may be less concerned with team members' lives as a whole. However, Kotter does believe that motivation and hunger are important for the team. For Kotter, the main key to motivation that endures is elevating and celebrating short-term wins.

Kotter says that each short-term win helps drive transformation in six ways:[11]

1. Provides evidence that the work is worth it. This helps each team member know that their sacrifice is important.
2. Rewards the team with encouragement that they are really doing it. Such positive reinforcement builds morale and motivation.
3. Helps clarify vision and strategy. These wins provide data on what's working and proof of concept.
4. Undermines critics and naysayers. When the transformation does what we promised, it becomes harder and harder to resist the promised change.
5. Keeps staff on board. Wins help those in the organizational hierarchy see that it's working and that it's worth it.
6. Builds momentum. Everyone loves to succeed and wants to be a part of a winning team.

Elevating and celebrating short-term wins also help drive transformation for a CORE team in a church or ministry. To do this well, the team leader must proactively identify what short-term wins would look like and regularly stop and celebrate when those wins occur.

Refocusing Team Members with the Three Ds

The three Ds—discipline, discipling, and direction—are practical ways a team leader can encourage team members to focus while inspiring them to fight through the temptation to quit or slip back to their former way of life. These are stairs that provide footholds on the slippery slope. They provide measurable short-term wins that the team members can reach and then celebrate. Let's look at each one.

1. *Restore spiritual disciplines.* No matter how mature a disciple is, she needs to remain rooted in her relationship with Christ through spiritual disciplines. As every mature disciple can attest, there's a tendency to drift from one's own spiritual disciplines in order to make disciples. My friend Tony Miltenberger sums it up when he says, "If you're not dedicated to your disciplines, then you'll be destroyed by your distractions." Even disciplemaking can be a distraction if it's not fueled by an abiding relationship with Jesus. Help team members by asking about their time in the Word and in prayer. Don't simply ask if it's happening, ask what God is teaching them through those disciplines. Ask about how God is encouraging, challenging,

or simply caring for them during that time. Next, share from your own time with God. Reflect together, and lean into gratitude for who God is and for those He's entrusted to you.

2. *Refocus disciplemaking.* Ask each team member who he is discipling. Celebrate the fact that your team members are discipling! Listen well to their struggles, and find areas to encourage them in how they are investing in their disciples and in how God is using their gifts as they disciple. Since some of your team members may be discipling for the first time, expect them to make mistakes, to feel insecure, and to feel responsible for a disciple's lack of progress. Keep reminding them that the real win is that they are discipling. You might share your past (and current) disciplemaking mistakes with them. Don't forget to help them see the difference they are making in their disciples' lives! What they are doing is important! At the same time, keep training them so that they can disciple with greater and greater proficiency.

3. *Reflect on distance traveled.* This is the practice of contrasting the past with the present and then looking to the future together. When done regularly, it defangs discouragement. In moments of fatigue or despair, remembering just how far we've come renews our strength. CORE team leaders must lift the eyes of each person from their shoes to their Savior. It often sounds something like this: "Look at how far you have come! God is with you on this journey. So am I, and so is this team. I can see the difference you're making! You

are doing a great job staying focused on Him (disciplines), investing in others (discipling), and continuing as He leads (direction)."

By using the three Ds, leaders spotlight effort more than results. They focus the team on Jesus, discipling others, and the future. Each empowers individuals to endure in the battle for lasting transformation. Some members of the CORE team need these relational check-ins more than others, but it's the leader's job to make them a priority. Like every good shepherd, he must be close enough to the flock to know when one has strayed or when one is feeling ill.

Team Leader Emphases in This Stage

While team members need to focus on the three Ds, team leaders need to focus their leadership on three things:

1. *Set the example of resting and running.* Growth requires toggling back and forth between resting and running. Team leaders who, like Jesus, make their own rest a priority can help team members see their own need to rest. Don't be a team leader who acts like they never get tired!

2. *Reinforce and reward effort over results.* Remember:

   Low proficiency + poor results = I quit.

   Keep praising the efforts of the team. Their consistent effort and improvement will result in mastery, but only if they stay in the game!

3. *Train team members' weaknesses.* If you observe the negative results these inexperienced disciplemakers are facing, you can tailor your training so that they can address those results now and avoid them next time. Being a beginner isn't a sin—it's just part of the journey. As the more experienced disciplemaker, think strategically about practical behaviors they can implement to become more effective as they disciple others.

Throwing Out the Agenda

Pastor Matt noticed that his CORE team was limping along. They had been meeting every other week for nearly two years. Each person on the team was discipling someone, and while they were encouraged, they also seemed tired.

He first noticed how two team members bowed out of the team meeting hours before the team was scheduled to meet. They said things like "I'm just not feeling up to it" and "I forgot the meeting was tonight. I made other plans." A year previously, they were excited to meet and gained energy from the team meetings.

During the meeting, Pastor Matt asked the team, "How are we doing? How's your morale and motivation toward this team and disciplemaking?"

A couple of them said they had been feeling tired. After that, others felt safe to say that they had been feeling the same way. It confirmed what Pastor Matt thought.

He threw out the meeting agenda for that night and pivoted to talking about the importance of time with Jesus. He then had them partner up and share what had been going on in their lives and in their times with God. He reminded them that Jesus' commandment to love is what fueled the great commission.

Later, he talked with the team members individually. After finding that more rest was needed, he canceled the next meeting. At the following meeting, the team decided to cancel the next four meetings, but they committed to walking with each other during that time—checking in on each other and leaning into their disciplines. Pastor Matt encouraged them about the discipling they were doing and reminded them about the distance they had traveled as individuals.

Two months later, the team met. Pastor Matt noticed that their motivation had returned. Pastor Matt may have saved his CORE team by giving them that space.

Endurance Is Doable

The team leader must lead skillfully through this phase of the process to prevent team members from burning out and jumping out of the process altogether. Team members offering help to one another is a vital part of the process as well. They need each other. As they listen to one another's experiences and struggles, hearts are encouraged and grit grows.

CORE teams who endure to the end will reap the harvest they are fighting so hard to produce. Seeing the process through will give the team the power to move outward into the church culture and into the neighborhood as they partner with God to advance the Kingdom.

Reflection Questions

1. Why is it that people sometimes see a better way, move toward that better way, and yet still fail to finish? When have you done that?

2. How do you know when a new way has replaced your old way?

3. What are the three Ds? How do they help team members push past their weariness?

4. What will you need to remember as you help each CORE team member endure to the end?

5. Communicate what you've discovered to God. What next step is He asking you to take?

TACTICS FOR BUILDING YOUR CORE TEAM

We are kept from our goal not by obstacles but by a clear path to a lesser goal.
ROBERT BRAULT

Don't look at a CORE team as the latest program to cure whatever ails your church or ministry. It won't. Many programs come fully endorsed by authors, publishers, and others who can vouch for their effectiveness. With so many people standing behind these programs, leaders don't have to. If a program works, everyone celebrates and looks toward the next one. If it doesn't work, everyone looks toward the next one. Either way, there's always the next one.

If you believe that Jesus' way is the best way to make disciples and a movement of disciplemakers, then there is nothing left to move on to. You can adjust the method or improve your skill, but the big picture of reaching the lost, growing them to maturity, and sending them out to do the same is the unchanging call for all believers.

Building a CORE team establishes a strong foundation for a disciplemaking culture. Your ability to reach that goal is connected to your ability to model the lifestyle of a disciplemaker and to lead the team. Team building is also intertwined with the depth and commitment of the team members themselves.

Pastor Devin (see chapter 5) attempted to build a CORE team three times before he achieved his goal. The first attempts yielded a few disciplemakers each, but not a CORE team. Instead of giving up or moving on, Devin remained convinced of the need for a CORE team to be the foundation for disciplemaking in the church. So he tried again. One thing was sure: He wasn't going to go back to the program cycle of prepare, launch, grow, plateau, decline, and end. Each time, Devin led with more skill, and on his third try, he ended up with a strong team of disciplemakers. His commitment has allowed his church to move beyond the program cycle and establish the pulsating rhythm of growth and rest, growth and rest.

This chapter has practical tips to help you get started in building a CORE team. Now that you understand the concepts, let's get in the weeds and do it.

Tactics for CORE Team Development

Start with Prayer

I can't emphasize prayer enough. Building a CORE team can't happen without God moving. As individuals, we are insufficient to build a team or initiate change in another person, or even in ourselves. In fact, without Him, we "can do *nothing*" (John 15:5, emphasis added). Not only did Jesus pray all night before inviting His team, but He also stayed in contact with the Father the whole time He led them (John 5:19-30). We must strive to follow His example!

Who to Invite

As you begin to build a CORE team, keep in mind that your goal for this team is to build a culture of disciplemakers. It's not simply to raise up disciplemakers, and it's not to build more spiritual leaders for programs. Your goal is to create a team of disciplemakers who will help you build a disciplemaking culture.

With that in mind, think strategically. Pray and ask God to show you who to invite. It's important that your team be a cross section of your church. Include both genders, racially diverse members, and multiple generations of adults.

As you pray, ask God to show you those who are hungry for more of Him. Those who are hungry already take advantage of current opportunities, are willing to clear space in their schedules for more opportunities, and faithfully apply what they are learning to their lives. Hunger is the first and most important criterion. If there are more hungry people than you can include, select those who are relational influencers already.

I recommend not putting couples on the team for two reasons. First, it's more strategic to impact multiple households instead of one. If the marriage is strong, you can trust one spouse to tell the other what's happening on the team. Second, members of a couple naturally influence each other. Two on one team can create imbalance on the team, which can make leading more difficult.

For instance, if one misses for a family commitment, then it's likely both will. If one is struggling, it's likely that both will struggle. This isn't a hard rule, but generally, it's not a great idea.

How (and How Many) to Invite

Most CORE teams are four to twelve people. In deciding how many to have on your team, consider the size of the church. The most important factor is how many people a leader can relationally walk with throughout the process. Remember, the leader must track with each individual through an intentional conversation *at least once a month* (see chapter 6). Some team leaders invite another established disciplemaker onto the team to help with this role. Doing so can enable the team to be bigger.

Disciplemaking is relational, so your invitation needs to be relational as well. An email alone isn't enough. It's okay to begin with an email for clear and consistent communication, but at the end of the email, let each person know that you will call or schedule a face-to-face meeting to talk with them personally to process the decision with them and to answer any questions they might have. For a sample CORE team invitation, visit my website (https://www.justingravitt.com/invitation-letter).

What's the Rhythm of Team Meetings?

Typically, the CORE team meets every other week for ninety minutes over the course of about a year. The duration isn't fixed because the team is driven by outcomes, not by a book or other curriculum. (Remember, the goals of the team are to become a team and for each person to become a disciplemaker.) While some have effectively met weekly, a monthly rhythm hasn't proved effective.

Emphasize the Commitment, Not the Opportunity

It's true that what you recruit *to* is what you recruit *for*. If you recruit someone to a team that will be life-changing, fulfilling, and fun, that's what people will show up expecting. If you recruit someone to trust God to do something difficult but important, then they will expect that. Jesus invited people to take up their cross, to eat of His flesh and drink of His blood, and to come and die (Luke 9:23; John 6:53; 12:24). I'm not saying to leave out the benefits as you invite people—just be sure to highlight the commitment expected.

Develop a Team, Not a Group

As you move forward, expect that cultural forces will try to pull you back into consumeristic thinking that emphasizes a group rather than a team. As I mentioned in chapter 3, many people are so used to engaging as a group that they aren't used to the effort it takes to be on a team. As the leader, you should view yourself as a player-coach and treat members as the team they are. Team members are connected to the mission and to one another. Here are a few ideas to try that will be useful during the team development journey. They will help you discern whether you have a team or a group:

- After you've met for a few months, ask team members as they walk into the room to sit next to the person they've been encouraging lately. If you have a group, each person might look around as if he or she missed an assignment. If you have a team, each person will have someone in mind and be happy to sit next to that person. It's important to ask who *they* have been encouraging, because they can control their actions, not the actions of others.

- If someone has missed a meeting, when he shows up for the next meeting, ask who reached out to him to catch him up on what he missed. If you have a group, no one will have called him. If you have a team, someone made sure this team member was ready for what would come next. The responsibility for catching up is on both sides: The person who missed should also reach out to a teammate or the leader. Being a good teammate means helping catch others up.

- Develop a list of ten questions for the team to answer on paper during the team meeting. Include questions like these: *Which spouses of your teammates can you name? How many of your teammates can you name who have been struggling in the past two months or are trusting God in a difficult circumstance? How many of your teammates have you prayed for by name in the last week?* Questions like these help the team see what it means to be a team. One team reflected back to me, "So it sounds like you are asking us to actually love each other?" Yes, I am!

What about Curriculum, Application, and Accountability?

The curriculum you choose to use isn't nearly as important as how you use it. As soon as you introduce a curriculum, you'll notice the team will start to refer to themselves as a class, a group, or a study. You must be vigilant to correct that language when it slips out in the meetings. Do it with a smile on your face. "No, this isn't a _____. We are here with two main goals. First, to become disciplemakers, and second, to become a team."

Team members sometimes slip back into using the old maps very easily. That's why it's so important to immediately correct the language used. If it is not corrected, what exists as muscle memory will grow into conscious thought, and then into conscious words, and finally into actions. As long as the team meets together, the leader needs to communicate the team's vision and objectives.

No matter what curriculum you choose, make sure you are making applications each time. I like to use the SMART acronym—Specific, Measurable, Attainable, Relevant to a spiritual need, and Time sensitive—to bring shape to applications. Each time you come together, refer back to each person's application as a way to build accountability. Most groups don't make applications; many who do never talk about them again. Transformation happens when applications are repeatedly made and implemented.

Any solid disciplemaking resource can be fruitful in the right hands. Choose one for the team. A few of my favorites when building a team like this are *The Ways of the Alongsider* by Bill Mowry, *The Master Plan of Evangelism* by Robert E. Coleman, and Paul's first letter to the Thessalonians.

When Does the CORE Team End?

Once you have a CORE team, don't end it. I've learned the hard way that ending a CORE team will also end hard-fought cultural gains as well. That doesn't mean the CORE team members have made a lifetime commitment. I encourage team leaders to provide regular off-ramps for team members after the first year. These off-ramps are typically at six-month or one-year intervals.

When a team member is ready to exit the team, she is responsible to find her replacement. In a culture of disciplemaking, there should be no shortage of disciplemakers interested in joining the team. It's important to communicate that if team members have the passion and interest to remain on the team, there is no need for them to leave it.

How to Bring a New Member onto the Team

Bringing a new team member onto the CORE team is an opportunity for the team to demonstrate the relational nature of disciplemaking, to celebrate the journey thus far, and to communicate the vision of the team. To do this well, the leader should prepare the *team* to lead the first meeting for the new person. Doing this regularly helps establish and reestablish the culture of the CORE team that is being exported to the greater culture. These are usually very encouraging meetings for the new person and everyone else.

What about People Who Feel Excluded?

For some leaders, the idea of having an invitation-only team feels risky. An internal struggle begins when they imagine the outrage of those who weren't asked to participate. This very rarely happens. Building a team of disciplemakers requires prayerful discernment of who to invite. Jesus chose to invite a team of twelve, and within that team was an inner three. Scripture gives us one scene of the disciples jockeying for position within the Twelve, but instead of protecting their feelings, Jesus challenged them to act as servants— putting others before themselves.[1] In the same way, we can't allow the fear of hurt feelings to keep us from developing a CORE team. Seldom does the selection process cause discernible problems for the pastor.

Can the CORE Team Approach Work for Large Churches or Ministries?

Yes. However, just as bigger buildings need bigger and deeper foundations, disciplemaking foundations for large ministries demand more time, energy, and people because disciplemaking is relational and always takes time. If you are only sending one team of ten into a culture of three thousand, that will take longer than if you send five or six teams. So the bigger the church, the more CORE teams are needed to impact that culture in a reasonable amount of time. A good rule of thumb is to have one CORE team of around ten for every 500–750 people (as measured by average weekly adult attendance).

To accomplish this, large churches or ministries need to prepare and equip disciplemaking staff to lead teams. The teams can start on the same date and, if possible, meet on the same day and at the same time. This allows the teams to connect on the way in and out and, in a sense, to partner together. Periodic relational events should also be included so that the teams can mix and connect. The path of multiple teams requires more coordination, but developing a larger and deeper foundation is always more work!

Reflection Questions

1. How does a leader start a CORE team?

2. When you invite people to join a CORE team, what should you remember?

3. How will you help CORE team members develop action steps or accountability?

4. Who will help you lead the CORE team(s) by reminding you of what you've outlined from earlier chapters' questions?

5. Communicate what you've discovered to God. What next step is He asking you to take?

PERSEVERANCE IS REQUIRED, NOT PERFECTION

She was unstoppable. Not because she did not have failures or doubts but because she continued on despite them.

BEAU TAPLIN

Recently, I shared a meal with Pastor Joe. For over a year, I've been helping him learn how to make disciplemakers. Lately, we've been talking about developing a disciplemaking foundation for his church. He asked me to paint him a picture of what a CORE team looks like. For the next twenty minutes, I unpacked for him much of what I've written in this book. As I spoke, I could see him catching the vision of the type of team that I was describing. That look of "getting it" made me speak with even more excitement and conviction. Not only was I painting Joe a picture, but I was adding color and flair to each aspect of building a CORE team. When I finally finished, Joe nodded and said plainly, "That sounds so intimidating. I don't think I could ever do it."

Perhaps you've felt like Joe while reading this book. As I've stated before, building a disciplemaking foundation is difficult—very difficult. But it's also doable. What I've described in this book is the ideal. In baseball terms, it's a perfect game.

A perfect game in baseball is when none of the batters reaches the base for the entire game. No hits, no walks, no hit batters, and no errors. They are incredibly rare. Since 1869, nearly 250,000 major league baseball games have been played.[1] Of those, only twenty-four of them were perfect games. No pitcher has ever pitched more than one perfect game. In a perfect game, not only does the pitcher have to be amazing, but his teammates must play perfect defense as well.

Though perfect games are rare, each time the umpire shouts, "Play ball!" a perfect game is possible.

For a baseball team, the goal isn't a perfect game; the goal is to win the game. As you build your disciplemaking foundation, keep in mind that the goal is a disciplemaking culture, not perfection. The process of building a CORE team takes time. Don't mistake obstacles for a crooked-tower moment (see chapter 1). Instead, pay attention to each step in building your CORE team. Remember that the outcome isn't entirely in your control. When obstacles come, continue the work, and trust that God is going to develop a team that can facilitate and support a culture of disciplemaking.

A well-laid foundation is worth everything it takes to develop it. Ministries that have a CORE team are able to build a disciplemaking culture that stands the tests of time and adversity. When a culture shifts, members of a CORE team are able to lean on one another and on God as they adapt accordingly.

When an individual falls, the team can respond appropriately by picking that person up or by drawing in someone else who is a better fit (like the disciples selected Matthias to replace Judas; see Acts 1:12-26).

A solid foundation allows a leader to be one of several who carry the burden of disciplemaking, embody the vision, and inspire others to join the mission. So go ahead—follow Jesus and the apostle Paul by laying a foundation that will ensure long-term stability for your disciplemaking culture!

To most, building a straight eight-story tower in Pisa, Italy, in the twelfth century would have seemed impossible. Though Bonanno Pisano had the courage to try, the sheer difficulty of the task surely caused him to question himself. Unfortunately for him, his crooked-tower moment led him to retreat in shame. But imagine if he could see the tower today.

Imagine him and John Burland looking at the tower together. Burland is the expert who led a team to stabilize the tower. The work took over ten years—more than twice as long as Pisano had worked on it.[2] Burland's team removed soil from the north side, installed a complex system of tunnels and wells to drain water, and connected heavy chains to the original foundation remnants and to the tower. They completed their work in 2001, and the tower has shown no signs of vulnerability since.

In 1989, Burland told the press, "No matter how many calculations we made, the tower should not have been standing at all. The height and weight coupled with the porous soil meant it should have fallen centuries ago."[3]

I love the thought of Pisano and Burland looking at the tower together. Pisano would be astounded that the tower is still standing . . . and he'd wonder who finished it! Burland would want to hear about Pisano's process for laying the foundation. As they talked, Pisano's shame would shift. He'd see how impressed this highly educated man was with his tower. I can almost hear Burland saying, "You really created a masterpiece, Bonanno!"

Ironically, the soil conditions that made it so vulnerable are the same conditions that protected it for centuries from earthquakes and other environmental variants. The building vibrates less because of the combination of the tower's height and rigidity and the softness of the soil.[4] What Pisano left behind as a failure became one of the world's most iconic buildings.

Most church leaders inherit a foundation that was laid long ago. The cracks in that foundation, if any exist, are obvious from the inside: declining attendance, cultural isolation, and lack of societal impact. Each one bears witness to the foundation problem underneath. From the outside, the problem is even clearer. After all, a lean is most evident to those outside the building. They see religiosity divorced from application, dogma divorced from compassion, and the proclamation of life where decay is evident. It's not that the skeptics have less need for Christ; but in many churchgoers the skeptics see the lean, not the One who draws all people to Himself (John 12:32).

The lean in the American church can't be ignored. Our culture continues to disciple people away from the church and scriptural truths. Our foundation problems must be addressed. If they aren't, the lean will just get worse.

Despite the challenges, I'm hopeful, because now, more than ever, there is a growing movement of Christian leaders—the church's architects and engineers—who are no longer satisfied with providing emotional experiences that don't lead to transformation, education that doesn't lead to action, and action that doesn't lead to reproduction. As I've discussed in this book, such a foundation is laid by a disciplemaking leader who is committed to becoming like Jesus and who develops a CORE team of disciplemakers. It requires a common vision as well as an unwavering commitment to the ways of God and to relating to one another through conflicts as each member works to endure. Disciplemaking cultures are built from such a team of committed disciples.[5]

Most of all, I'm hopeful because just as the Leaning Tower of Pisa was protected and supported by the soil, so too is the church. Jesus is the very ground into which any foundation is laid. My confidence is in Him and in His heart to protect and support the church as it overcomes the world. In His grace, He takes what we offer and makes it enough. He accepts our faults and blind spots and helps us progress.

So let's commit to building a foundation from Jesus' example with His disciples. All you need is a commitment to walk with Him and to avoid giving up when obstacles come. Apart from Him, you can do nothing. But with Him, you can do even greater things than He did![6]

Reflection Questions

1. What current foundation does your church/ministry have in disciplemaking? Is there a team? Do people know who is on the team?

2. As you reflect on Pisano's journey with the Leaning Tower of Pisa, what can you learn from his mistakes?

3. Write a paragraph on why it's important to lay a disciplemaking foundation before trying to build a disciplemaking culture.

4. Write a few paragraphs on what you have learned from this book and what you will do as a result.

5. Tell someone else what you are committing to do. Ask that person to hold you accountable within a specific time frame.

6. Communicate what you've discovered to God. What next step is He asking you to take?

Definitions

CORE Team: A group of people who have a Common vision, Own that vision individually, are Relationally resilient as a result of their connection to one another and the mission, and have the Endurance to weather discouragement, weariness, and hardship in order to reach their objective. The CORE team has two primary goals: (1) to become a team, and (2) for each person to become a disciplemaker. The purpose in reaching those goals is so that the team can impact the greater church/ministry culture. However, the ultimate purpose is to glorify God.

Culture: A population's way of life. It includes the shared language, beliefs, values, stories, history, practices, and habits of a people. It's what most of the people believe, think, and do most of the time. It forms the (mostly invisible) operating system for that population.

Disciple: Someone who follows Jesus in order to become just like Jesus, is being changed by Jesus, and is committed to the mission of Jesus.

Disciplemaker/Discipler/Reproducing Disciple/Multiplying Disciple/Laborer: A disciple who is motivated by Christological, covenantal, or missional aims to help at least one other disciple become like Jesus by following Jesus, being changed by Jesus, and joining the mission of Jesus. Being a disciplemaker is marked by relationship, intentionality, and mission, and it continues until that disciple becomes an experienced disciplemaker.

Disciplemaking: A specific type of relationship carried out by people who are primarily motivated by Christological, covenantal, or missional aims, using Jesus' methods that are relational, intentional, and missional. The relationship leads to fruit that multiplies in the form of new disciples, new disciplemakers, and momentum in three dimensions: (1) out toward the lost, (2) in toward the church, and (3) down into the life of the individual disciple.

Disciplemaking Culture: A population who has intentionally formed an identity around being disciples of Jesus and making disciples using the methods of Jesus. Disciplemaking is a key part of the culture's DNA.

Discipleship: The process of helping a disciple grow to Christlike maturity—minus intentional movement toward making other disciples.

Foundation of a Disciplemaking Culture: A CORE team of disciplemakers who choose to allow their lives to be dynamic examples of what it means to follow Jesus. The team's collective and individual examples proclaim to the culture that embracing Jesus' gospel call to "follow Me" leads to a transformed life.

Jesus-Style Disciplemaking: Disciplemaking that seeks to replicate in today's world the principles used by Jesus in making disciples. There is wide agreement that the principles in *The Master Plan of Evangelism* by Robert E. Coleman are a reliable guide for Jesus' disciplemaking methods.

The Coaching Conversation

A useful skill in disciplemaking is the coaching conversation. This intentional conversation follows a pattern that helps a person unlock his or her desires and move toward set goals. Coaching conversations are built upon questions and follow a broad pattern that identifies the desired future, the current reality, action steps, barriers, and boosts. Each aspect is powerful in helping a person move from mired to motivated.

Coaching uses skillful conversations to bring focus to transformation. It doesn't take much for a disciplemaker to develop a coaching approach. Instead of always teaching or telling, ask. A careful study of Jesus' life makes it clear that asking questions was one of the primary ways Jesus taught others. Coaching provides a framework for those questions and allows space for the disciple to consider their own course of action.

Below is a coaching framework based on certain categories of questions. To help you remember these, think in terms of the bridge I mentioned in chapter 6. You stand on a cliff looking across to the desired future, then at your current reality. Next, you think about how you will get over there and what barriers could disrupt your plans. Finally, you think about what you learned through the entire process.

Below are sample questions for each category that you can use as you develop your own coaching approach in disciplemaking.

Desired Future
- What do you want to happen with _____?
- Why do you want to see that happen?
- What does success look like for you in this area?
- What motivates you to move forward in this area?
- How would success in this area change your life?

Current Reality
- How would you describe where you are now?
- What are a few steps that you could take to move forward?
- What have you already tried?
- What are some other choices or options?
- What is the cost of not doing anything?

Action Steps
- What needs to happen for you to achieve your goal?
- What else might you try?
- Which of those options is the most important to do now?
- When can you begin to implement those plans?
- Is there anything these action steps are leaving out?

Barriers

- What do you need in order to follow through with these actions?
- What roadblocks do you expect? How will you get through them?
- How can your faith in God's power or Scripture help you as you move forward?
- Who else can you invite to help hold you accountable or encourage you?
- Is there anything else you will need to be successful?

Recap

- What commitments are you making today?
- In what ways do you sense God at work in these things?
- What small wins can you anticipate as you move forward?
- Is there anything else you need from me right now?
- What did you learn today from our conversation?

Gratitudes

I need to start with my gratitude to Bobby Harrington for inviting me to write an e-book for Discipleship.org in 2019. Thank you for (graciously) rejecting my first attempt and allowing me to try again, which led to the e-book *The Foundation of a Disciplemaking Culture*.

I'm grateful for all my local readers of the first draft of the e-book. Ken Cecil, Kristen Gravitt, Scott Hoefler, Dave Holmes, Seth Jump, Tony Miltenberger, Paul Pyle, Doug Sonnenberg, and Mike Tuttle: Thank you for taking the time to read it and for the invaluable feedback you provided.

I'm grateful for friends who encouraged me to cultivate the e-book into a more complete book. I believe many will be helped as a result. Duane Sherman, Dane Allphin, Don Pape, Chad Harrington, Dennis Blevins, and Bill Mowry: Thank you. Your encouragement made all the difference some days.

I'm grateful to NavPress and Tyndale for their partnership in making this book. Dave Zimmerman, Elizabeth Schroll, Linda Washington, Robin Bermel, and Jessica Adams: Thank you for your work in improving the book and getting it into the hands of those we're serving together.

I'm grateful for those who have partnered with me and who continue to do so. Thank you to the Dayton Disciple Makers Network, Navigators Church Ministries, Discipleship.org, and The Navigators at large. Serving with you has helped me grow and mature in immeasurable ways.

I'm grateful for those who have intentionally and directly invested in my spiritual development over the years. Jeff Gravitt, Greg Bryan, Rich Jarvi, Bruce and Rosie Das, Allen Busenitz, George McBride, and Bill Mowry: Thank you for taking the time to help me mature in the faith.

I'm grateful for my family. Thank you to my grandparents and my mother for your care and nurture. I miss you all very much. Thank you to my dad, whose friendship and continued influence are so appreciated. Thank you to my wife, Kristen, whose love and support mean the world to me. And thank you to my children for your excitement about this book. You constantly remind me to live with joy!

Most of all, I'm grateful to God, from whom all blessings come. Thank You for loving me in spite of who I have been—and who I am. Thank You for drawing me close day by day and for constantly teaching me that Your way is best.

Notes

PREFACE

1. Matthew 9:37, ESV. The NIV has *workers*.
2. Disciplemaking stories are true throughout. Names have been changed to preserve privacy.

CHAPTER 1 | FOUNDATION PROBLEMS

1. *Merriam-Webster*, s.v. "disciple," accessed June 12, 2023, https://www.merriam-webster.com/dictionary/disciple.
2. Luke 19:10.
3. Mark Dever, *Discipling* (Wheaton, IL: Crossway, 2016), 17.
4. Matthew 28:19-20.
5. Matthew 28:19-20; Mark 16:15; Luke 24:47; John 20:21; Acts 1:8.
6. Mark 4:27-29; 1 Corinthians 3:7; Philippians 1:6; 2:13.
7. See John 15:5, NKJV.
8. Philippians 1:6; 2:13; 2 Peter 1:3-4.
9. Luke 6:40; 1 Corinthians 11:1; 1 Peter 2:21; 1 John 2:6.
10. Robert E. Coleman, *The Master Plan of Evangelism* (Old Tappan, NJ: Fleming H. Revell Company, 1963).
11. Coleman's eight principles are Selection, Association, Consecration, Impartation, Demonstration, Delegation, Supervision, and Reproduction.
12. Luke 19:10.
13. Ephesians 4:12.

CHAPTER 2 | BUILD A DISCIPLEMAKING CULTURE?

1. Walter Lippmann, *A Preface to Politics* (New York: Mitchell Kennerley, 1913), 306.

2. John 17:4-23.
3. See, for example, Matthew 28:19-20; Luke 6:40; 1 Peter 2:21; 1 John 2:6.
4. See 1 Corinthians 3:10-13.

CHAPTER 3 | THE CORE TEAM AS THE FOUNDATION

1. Most scholars believe that John 1–4 covers roughly the first year of Jesus' ministry. John is likely the unnamed disciple in those chapters.
2. Robert L. Thomas and Stanley N. Gundry, *A Harmony of the Gospels* (Chicago: Moody Press, 1978); A. T. Robertson, *A Harmony of the Gospels for Students of the Life of Christ* (New York: George H. Doran Company, 1922).
3. 1 Thessalonians 1:1, 5.
4. 1 Thessalonians 1:7-8.
5. Ephesians 4:11-13.
6. John P. Kotter bio, Harvard Business School, accessed June 12, 2023, https://www.hbs.edu/faculty/Pages/profile.aspx?facId=6495.
7. "The 25 Most Influential Business Management Books," *Time*, n.d., accessed April 19, 2024, https://content.time.com/time/specials/packages/completelist/0,29569,2086680,00.html.
8. John P. Kotter, *Leading Change* (Boston: Harvard Business School Press, 1996), 6, emphasis added.
9. Kotter, *Leading Change*, 51–52, emphasis added.

CHAPTER 4 | DISCIPLEMAKER AS LEAD BUILDER

1. "The Foundation of the Leaning Tower of Pisa," Ram Jack, September 22, 2015, https://www.ramjack.com/houston/about/news-events/2015/september/the-foundation-of-the-leaning-tower-of-pisa.
2. Joe Pinkstone, "Leaning Tower of Pisa's Architect Is Revealed: Bonanno Pisano Designed the Monument in the 12th Century but Was Embarrassed by Its Tilt, Experts Claim," *Daily Mail*, December 19, 2019, https://www.dailymail.co.uk/sciencetech/article-7809335/Leaning-Tower-Pisas-architect-revealed-Bonanno-Pisano.html.
3. Pinkstone, "Leaning Tower of Pisa's Architect Is Revealed."
4. "In U.S., Decline of Christianity Continues at Rapid Pace," Pew Research Center, October 17, 2019, https://www.pewforum.org/2019/10/17/in-u-s-decline-of-christianity-continues-at-rapid-pace.
5. Justin Nortey and Michael Rotolo, "How the Pandemic Has Affected Attendance at U.S. Religious Services," Pew Research Center, March 28, 2023, https://www.pewresearch.org/religion/2023/03/28/how-the-pandemic-has-affected-attendance-at-u-s-religious-services.

6. Daniel Silliman, "Decline of Christianity Shows No Signs of Stopping," *Christianity Today*, September 13, 2022, https://www.christianitytoday .com/news/2022/september/christian-decline-inexorable-nones-rise-pew -study.html.

7. Thom S. Rainer, "Why Your Church Has to Replace 32 Percent of Its Attendance to Stay Even Each Year," Church Answers, January 23, 2023, https://churchanswers.com/blog/why-your-church-has-to-replace-32 -percent-of-its-attendance-to-stay-even-each-year.

8. Ralph Martin Novak, *Christianity and the Roman Empire: Background Texts* (Harrisburg, PA: Trinity Press International, 2001), 167–69.

9. C. S. Lewis, *Mere Christianity* (New York: Harper One, 2015), 199–200.

10. Tony Morgan, "How Much Should Churches Spend on Their Church Staff?," The Unstuck Group, July 11, 2022, https://theunstuckgroup.com /how-much-should-churches-spend-on-their-staff.

11. Matthew Branaugh, "How Churches Spend Their Money," Church Law and Tax, July 15, 2014, https://www.churchlawandtax.com/manage-finances /budgets/how-churches-spend-their-money.

12. Steve Law, "Budget Percentages," Finance for Churches, September 12, 2011, https://financeforchurches.org/budget-percentages.

13. Alice Matagora, *How to Save the World: Disciplemaking Made Simple* (Colorado Springs: NavPress, 2022), 22.

14. John 5:19; 17:6.

15. Matthew 4:19.

16. Luke 5:31-32.

17. Mark 3:15.

18. Matthew 28:19-20; Acts 1:8.

19. Luke 5:31-32.

20. Jeffery Fulks, Randy Petersen, and John Farquhar Plake, *State of the Bible USA 2023*, American Bible Society, December 2023, https://1s712.american bible.org/state-of-the-bible/stateofthebible/State_of_the_bible-2023.pdf, 6.

21. Ephesians 4:11-16; Colossians 1:28-29.

22. Matthew 28:18-20.

23. John 14:12.

24. Revelation 7:9.

25. Galatians 3:29.

26. Genesis 15:5-6; 26:2-6; 28:13-15.

27. Acts 13:36.

28. 2 Corinthians 1:20; 2 Peter 1:4.

29. Matthew 28:18-20.

30. Hebrews 12:1.

31. Mark 10:46-52; Luke 18:35-42.

32. Mark 5:1-20.

33. Mark 2:1-12; Luke 5:18-26.

34. Matthew 9:35-36.

35. Matthew 9:36.

36. Mark 1:17; Luke 19:10; John 2:23-25; 6:25-71; 17:6-10.

37. Gervase R. Bushe and Robert J. Marshak, eds., *Dialogic Organization Development: The Theory and Practice of Transformational Change* (Oakland, CA: Berrett-Koehler Publishers, 2015), 84.

38. John P. Kotter, *Leading Change* (Boston: Harvard Business School Press, 1996), 4.

39. John P. Kotter, "Management Is (Still) Not Leadership," *Harvard Business Review*, January 9, 2013, https://hbr.org/2013/01/management-is-still-not-leadership.

40. J. Stewart Black, *It Starts with One*, 3rd ed. (Upper Saddle River, NJ: Pearson Education, 2014), 1–3.

CHAPTER 5 | COMMON VISION

1. "California as an Island in Maps," Stanford Libraries, accessed June 12, 2023, https://exhibits.stanford.edu/california-as-an-island.

2. Ken Jennings, "For Centuries, Europeans Thought California Was an Island," Condé Nast Traveler, March 19, 2018, https://www.cntraveler.com/story/for-centuries-europeans-thought-california-was-an-island.

3. Wikipedia, s.v. "Island of California," last modified April 2, 2024, 18:24, https://en.wikipedia.org/wiki/Island_of_California.

4. Greg Miller, "18 Maps from When the World Thought California Was an Island," WIRED, April 18, 2014, https://www.wired.com/2014/04/maps-california-island.

5. Ned Pennant-Rea, "Maps Showing California as an Island," May 15, 2018, *The Public Domain Review*, https://publicdomainreview.org/collection/maps-showing-california-as-an-island.

6. Bill Hull and Ben Sobels, *The Discipleship Gospel: What Jesus Preached—We Must Follow* (Nashville: HIM Publications, 2018), 24.

7. James 2:14-24.

8. Martin Luther, *A Commentary on St. Paul's Epistle to the Galatians*, trans. Theodore Graebner, Christian Classics Ethereal Library, accessed April 19, 2024, https://www.ccel.org/ccel/luther/galatians.viii.html. See especially Luther's commentary on Galatians 5:6.

9. Bill Hull, *Conversion and Discipleship* (Nashville: Zondervan, 2016); Hull and Sobels, *The Discipleship Gospel*.

10. Ecclesiastes 3:11.
11. Bill Hull in a presentation to the Navigators staff on November 9, 2019.
12. Matthew 5:21-44; Luke 9:23.
13. John 13:6.
14. John P. Kotter, *Leading Change* (Boston: Harvard Business School Press, 1996), 68–69.
15. Patrick Lencioni, *The Advantage* (San Francisco: Jossey-Bass Publications, 2012), 77.

CHAPTER 6 | OWNED INDIVIDUALLY

1. Glenn Clark, *The Man Who Talks with the Flowers: The Story of George Washington Carver* (Eastford, CT: Martino Fine Books, 2011), 20.
2. Bill Catlette and Richard Hadden, *Contented Cows Give Better Milk* (Germantown, TN: Saltillo Press, 2001), 88.
3. J. Stewart Black, *It Starts with One*, 3rd ed. (Upper Saddle River, NJ: Pearson Education, 2014), 98, 107.
4. Matthew 4:19; Mark 3:14.
5. John P. Kotter, *Leading Change* (Boston: Harvard Business School Press, 1996), 9.
6. Kotter, *Leading Change*, 5.
7. Black, *It Starts with One*, 1.

CHAPTER 7 | RELATIONALLY RESILIENT

1. Original Design Challenge, "Peter Skillman Marshmallow Design Challenge," January 27, 2014, YouTube video, 3:31, https://www.youtube.com/watch?v=1p5sBzMtB3Q.
2. Tom Wujec, "Build a Tower, Build a Team," filmed February 2010, TED video, 6:35, https://www.ted.com/talks/tom_wujec_build_a_tower_build_a_team?language=en.
3. Wujec, "Build a Tower, Build a Team."
4. Daniel Coyle, *The Culture Code* (New York, Bantam Books, 2018), xvii.
5. "106 Divorce Statistics You Can't Ignore: 2023 Divorce Rates and Impact on Children," FinancesOnline, accessed June 12, 2023, https://financesonline.com/divorce-statistics.
6. John 13:34-35.
7. Neil Paine et al., "2014 NBA Preview: The Rise of the Warriors," FiveThirtyEight, October 24, 2014, https://fivethirtyeight.com/features/2014-nba-preview-the-rise-of-the-warriors.
8. Coyle, *Culture Code*, 52.
9. Matthew 5:9.

10. See also Matthew 18:1-5; Luke 9:46-48.
11. John P. Kotter, *Leading Change* (Boston: Harvard Business School Press, 1996), 55.
12. Kotter, *Leading Change*, 61.
13. Kotter, *Leading Change*, 61.

CHAPTER 8 | ENDURE TO THE END
1. Mark 1:38; Luke 8:38-39.
2. Matthew 28:17.
3. Mark 3:14.
4. John 15:15.
5. John 13:34; 15:15.
6. Carl W. Wilson, *With Christ in the School of Disciple Building* (Colorado Springs: NavPress, 2009), 178–79.
7. Hebrews 12:2.
8. Dann Spader, *4 Chair Discipling*, (Chicago: Moody Publishers, 2014), 89.
9. John 17:6-20.
10. John 14:12; 16:7, 12-15, 24.
11. John P. Kotter, *Leading Change* (Boston: Harvard Business School Press, 1996), 123.

CHAPTER 9 | TACTICS FOR BUILDING YOUR CORE TEAM
1. Matthew 20:20-28.

CONCLUSION | PERSEVERANCE IS REQUIRED, NOT PERFECTION
1. 238,500 as of 2022, per Wikipedia, s.v. "List of Major League Baseball perfect games," last modified April 20, 2024, 05:29, https://en.wikipedia.org/wiki/List_of_Major_League_Baseball_perfect_games.
2. Barbie Latza Nadeau, "Leaning Tower of Pisa Corrects Itself... a Little," *Scientific American*, November 30, 2018, https://www.scientificamerican.com/article/leaning-tower-of-pisa-corrects-itself-a-little.
3. Matt Hickman, "The Leaning Tower of Pisa Is Leaning a Bit Less These Days," Treehugger, updated December 7, 2018, https://www.treehugger.com/leaning-tower-pisa-leaning-bit-less-these-days-4868726#.
4. Doyle Rice, "Why Doesn't the Leaning Tower of Pisa Fall Over?," *USA Today*, updated May 16, 2018, https://www.usatoday.com/story/news/world/2018/05/10/leaning-tower-pisa-why-still-standing/598673002.
5. Matthew 28:18-20; Luke 6:40; Ephesians 4:11-13.
6. John 14:12.

About the Author

Justin Gravitt is a disciplemaking leader and writer whose primary passion is to help everyday believers repurpose their lives in light of God's plan for them as disciplemakers. Justin has served with The Navigators since 2000 and is the founder and executive director of the Dayton Disciple Makers Network as well as the host of the popular *Practitioners' Podcast*. He's an avid Reds fan who loves the beach and dad-joking his kids. Justin lives in Dayton, Ohio, with his wife, Kristen, and their four children. To connect with him or to learn more, visit his website at justingravitt.com.

NavPress is the book-publishing arm of The Navigators.

Since 1933, The Navigators has helped people around the world bring hope and purpose to others in college campuses, local churches, workplaces, neighborhoods, and hard-to-reach places all over the world, face-to-face and person-by-person in an approach we call Life-to-Life® discipleship. We have committed together to know Christ, make Him known, and help others do the same.®

Would you like to join this adventure of discipleship and disciplemaking?

- Take a Digital Discipleship Journey at **navigators.org/disciplemaking**.
- Get more discipleship and disciplemaking content at **thedisciplemaker.org**.
- Find your next book, Bible, or discipleship resource at **navpress.com**.

 @NavPressPublishing

 @NavPress

 @navpressbooks